# Trade and Capital Flow among Asian Economies

Trade and capital are important in the Asia region. Trade in the APEC region has been increasing, but the large rise in China's exports has also been disturbing as it exhibits export substitution. The first two chapters conclude that every economy has gained in trade, though some are more successful than others. Furthermore that rise in export has a lot to do with a rise in foreign direct investments. Macroeconomic stability is the pre-condition to growth. Empirical studies show that the lack of stability has encouraged capital to flee an economy. Similarly, a market-oriented, price-driven and matured financial market provides an alternative source of funding. The lesson in economic development is that success in economic growth requires both an externally friendly market environment as well as consistent and favourable internal policies.

Overview of rest of contributions:
Other contributions cover private sector development in China, impacts on management and business in Korea and industrialisation in Hong Kong.

This book was previously published as a special issue of *Asia Pacific Business Review.*

**Chris Rowley** is a Professor at the Cass Business School at City University, London, and is Editor of the journal Asia Pacific Business Review. He is also a member of the Editorial Board of several leading international journals. He has consultancy experience with unions, business enterprises and government departments and is a respected author of over 230 publications.

T0333866

# Trade and Capital Flow among Asian Economies

## Issues and Developments in Business and Management

Edited by
Chris Rowley

Routledge
Taylor & Francis Group

LONDON AND NEW YORK

First published 2009 by Routledge
2 Park Square, Milton Park, Abingdon, Oxon, OX14 4RN

Simultaneously published in the USA and Canada by Routledge
52 Vanderbilt Avenue, New York, NY 10017

First issued in paperback 2018

*Routledge is an imprint of the Taylor & Francis Group, an informa business*

*British Library Cataloguing in Publication Data*
A catalogue record for this book is available from the British Library

Typeset in Times 11/12pt by Alden Prepress Services, Northampton

ISBN 13: 978-1-138-99373-0 (pbk)
ISBN 13: 978-0-415-44553-5 (hbk)

MIX
Paper from
responsible sources
FSC
www.fsc.org   FSC™ C013985

Printed in the United Kingdom
by Henry Ling Limited

# CONTENTS

# Changing Patterns of Trade, Capital and Management Across Asian Economies

## CHRIS ROWLEY

This volume concentrates on Asia's capital markets, foreign direct investment (FDI), trade and industry, management and the performance of individual economic development in varied Asian economies. The countries covered in include those in both South East Asia, such as Thailand, Malaysia, Indonesia and the Philippines and also North East Asia, such as Japan, Korea, China (and Hong Kong), These are analysed in a variety of ways and in a usefully comparative and historically grounded fashion.

The first chapter, by Edsel L. Bela, Jr., looks at the problem of so-called 'capital flee' from the four Association of the South East Asian Nations (ASEAN) economies of Thailand, Indonesia, Malaysia and the Philippines in the period from 1970 to 2002. The issue in this chapter is not so much the success and failure in export and trade in these four economies, but the degree of instability that has encouraged this capital flee, which reduced potential domestic growth. The lesson from the capital fleeing experience of these four economies is the need to maintain macroeconomic stability that attracts FDI, as well as avoiding hard earned capital leaving the country, thereby depriving domestic growth potential. Macroeconomic stability helps to build up a virtuous cycle, while capital flee leads to a vicious cycle.

The second chapter by Ito and Yoshida, is more focused on the triangular trade relationship between the US, Japan and China. The chapter arises from the trade substitution assumption used to explain the rise in China's exports. The hypothesis is that the 'fall' in Japan's exports to the US has been made up by the rise in China's exports to the US. The rise in such exports has been the result of Japan's increase in FDI in China. The finding of the chapter basically reconfirms that China's rise in exports is largely due to the large absorption on foreign direct investment from Japan and other countries.

The third chapter poses a number of legal and institutional questions that have to be addressed in the area. The chapter makes three proposals on the policy framework towards the establishment of a market-oriented Asian debt market. Various fundamentals and institutional legalities are discussed in the chapter. It also points out that Asia is not short of capital, but 'its capability to apportion financial resources is pervasively suspect'. As an echo to capital fleeing, a well-established Asian debt market would provide an alternative source of finance among Asian economies.

The fourth chapter considers the development of the private sector in post-reform China, paying particular attention to the related development in the legal framework and the emergence of small- and medium-sized enterprises. With the establishment of the so-called township and village enterprises, the chapter notes the continued influence by the government at various levels. The discussion in the chapter is supported by primary data from interviews with directors from enterprises and local government officials. The chapter concludes favourably that the framework for private sector development in China has largely been established and that the economic activities of the private sector will grow.

The fifth chapter turns our attention to the management experience in key Korean business corporations. The chapter makes a distinction in the management style of Korean corporations between the pre- and post-Asian Financial Crisis of 1997 situation. The chapter elaborates on the management issues in relation to Korean industrialization and the importance of the *chaebol*, the indigenous family-founded and run, large, diversified corporations. In the era of Korean industrialization before 1997 the urge of the 'export drive' required a considerable amount of government involvement and support, but Western styles of management, as well as the use of management consultants, have been adopted since 1997.

The last chapter in this volume follows the Korean case and studies the labour-intensive industrialization experience in the Hong Kong economy during the 1950–1970 period. The data used is historical but only released recently from British files. Contrary to the view that labour-intensive industries have been the core business during Hong Kong's industrialization, the chapter shows that there was a dual strategy of using both labour-intensive and capital-intensive production techniques. The chapter also discusses the related issues in the Hong Kong economy during the period and also implications on the contemporary situation in Hong Kong.

The message one grabs after reading these six chapters is that a strong institutional establishment and a proper instituted legal framework are pre-requisites to good management, success in trade and industrial development. As such, the changing patterns of trade and capital flows across Asia should not been seen in conceptual, spatial or historical vacuum, but rather within the rich grounded context.

# Was Capital Fleeing Southeast Asia? Estimates from Indonesia, Malaysia, the Philippines, and Thailand

EDSEL L. BEJA JR.

## Introduction

The title states the objective of this article: we are interested in determining the level of capital flight from South-east Asia, in particular, Indonesia, Malaysia, the Philippines, and Thailand. The article covers the period 1970 to 2002.

To ask whether or not capital was fleeing South-east Asia may be a bit surprising at first glance. After all, Indonesia, Malaysia, Thailand, and to some extent, the Philippines, have had relatively high growth rates since the 1970s. Except perhaps for the Philippines, the other three countries had impressive growth rates from the 1980s to until, say, 1996. In fact, they were among the Asian 'miracle economies' identified in World Bank (1993). As data from the World Development Indicators show, the average growth rate between 1970 and 2002 was 6.1 per cent for Indonesia, 6.7 per cent for Malaysia, and 6.5 per cent for Thailand, while the Philippines had 3.6 per cent. Following conventional analysis, we expect capital to stay and, in fact, not flee these countries. In addition, external capital will be attracted to them.

But our research shows that these four south-east Asian countries experienced substantial capital flight between 1970 and 2002. Also, capital flight was especially large in the 1990s. As expected, high levels of capital flight occurred during periods of economic and political crises and instability. Yet there were also cases of high capital flight during periods of robust economic growth, which is indeed interesting and counter-intuitive. In this article, we do not present a reason for the flight of capital from the region because we have done so elsewhere (see, e.g. Beja, 2005). Here, we focus on the estimate and the magnitude of capital flight from the four countries. At this stage, the answer to the question posed in the title of this article is affirmative.

The article has nine sections. Following this introduction, a brief literature review on capital flight is presented. The theory of capital flight is then discussed, followed by the hypotheses of the article, and an analysis of data. The results are followed by implications for theory and policy, and for management and/or business, respectively.

## Literature Review

This section presents a brief review of the literature. Earlier studies suggest that capital flight is not a new issue. Kindleberger (1987), for example, documents capital flight from Europe and the United States in the early 20th century or, in the case of Europe, even during the 17th century and earlier. In the 1930s, and after the Second World War, there were concerns about capital flight from Europe to the United States. In fact, this was a subject of debate at the Bretton Woods meetings (see, e.g., Helleiner, 1994). In recent periods, studies have documented capital flight from the Organization of Economic Cooperation and Development (OECD) countries (see, e.g., Gibson & Tskalotos, 1993).

But capital flight is of particularly important concern for the developing countries for at least three reasons. The first is capital scarcity in developing countries, and capital flight adds to the problem. In addition, capital flight restricts their capacity and ability to mobilize domestic funds or access foreign resources. So, in addition to a wide range of negative impacts, capital flight contributes to retarding growth and development in developing countries. In other words, it contributes to underdevelopment.

Second, capital flight can lead to a negative feedback process, which is especially true during periods of crises, instability, and uncertainty. Then, as resource constraints become binding, there is the possibility of being cut off from external sources of funds, growth will be further limited. More capital flight could occur as a result. In this situation, economic policies become more difficult to implement and raising the social conditions of people become a heavier burden to address. In short, capital flight makes the twin goals of growth and development much more challenging to pursue. Thus, when developing countries are already lagging behind on the economic ladder, capital flight knocks them several rungs down. In this context, capital flight is an economic threat to the developing world.

A third reason concerns economic justice, in particular, the distributive impacts of external indebtedness and capital fight, as well as the legitimacy of external debt itself. When external debts are being squandered by the elite or inappropriately used to benefit only a few in the form of capital flight, the rest of society suffers. More importantly, the non-trivial economic costs of external indebtedness and capital flight are imposed on the majority of society. As such, we need to question the legitimacy of external debt itself and the rationale for continuing to honour debts that society on the whole did not benefit from.

Recent interest in capital flight was triggered by the 1980s Latin American debt crisis. At that time, there were two foci of research on capital flight. One was that scholars wanted to understand the relationship between capital flight and external debt because capital flight undermined the ability of highly indebted countries to repay or service their mounting external debts (see, e.g., Lessard & Williamson, 1987). The other focus was that scholars wanted to examine whether or not external debt fuels or propels capital flight, and vice versa (see, e.g., Boyce, 1992).

After the 1980s debt crises, flight of capital became less of an issue. In turn, capital started to flow back to the developing countries, perhaps with the exception of Africa (see, e.g., Collier *et al.*, 2004). Scholars stopped paying attention to capital flight. By the latter half of the 1990s, however, there was a resurgence of capital flight as developing countries faced more and intense financial and economic crises. Once again, scholars are re-examining the problem.

We argue that there are at least three reasons why a reconsideration of capital flight is needed today. The first reason is, as in the past, external debts. In particular, country indebtedness remains a big problem to developing countries, including Indonesia, the Philippines, and Thailand, but less so perhaps for Malaysia if we use a 50 per cent external debt to GDP ratio as the benchmark (Table 1). In fact, many developing countries are again becoming vulnerable to debt-related crises. Leung (2003), for example, finds empirical evidence that increased indebtedness is positively correlated with increased intensity and frequency of debt-related economic cycles, a problem that is especially significant in Africa. The 1997–98 Asian Crisis, for instance, was in part rooted in the accumulation of external debts, albeit private external debts. As in Boyce (1992), there remains a close link between capital flight and external debt.

Another reason relates to changes in the economic policies that have been adopted by or, in some cases, forced upon developing countries. In particular, neo-liberal economic policies led to aggressive deregulation and financial liberalization without ensuring, or in some cases neglecting, effective financial governance and administrative capacities. As such, developing economies became more vulnerable to financial swings, crises, and contagions (see, e.g., Eichengreen & Mussa, 1998; Furman & Stiglitz, 1998). In fact, some scholars argue that

**Table 1.** Share of total external debt to gdp, by region 1970–2002

| Region | 1970s | 1980s | 1990s | 2000s |
|---|---|---|---|---|
| Asia | 0.21 | 0.29 | 0.38 | 0.47 |
| Indonesia | 0.47 | 0.27 | 0.61 | 0.93 |
| Malaysia | 0.12 | 0.27 | 0.35 | 0.47 |
| Philippines | 0.33 | 0.54 | 0.69 | 0.67 |
| Thailand | 0.14 | 0.26 | 0.33 | 0.65 |
| Latin America | 0.21 | 0.35 | 0.60 | 0.47 |
| Africa | 0.19 | 0.42 | 0.83 | 1.05 |

*Source*: Global Development Finance (2004)

financial and economic crises are inevitable in such contexts (see, e.g., Palma, 2003). Other scholars maintain that these crises are necessary 'growing pains' associated with the process of deregulation and financial liberalization (see, e.g., Prasad *et al.*, 2003).

However, we stress that the longer a country remains in such a situation, and the longer it postpones the reintroduction of governance structures and administrative capacities, the higher are the chances that financial and economic crises occur. Moreover, crises will become more intense and their social and economic costs will be very significant. From this perspective, we argue that neo-liberal policies have made the developing world more vulnerable to capital flight. In addition, significant and volatile capital flight will be common in developing countries.

The third reason for reconsideration is that capital flight, as pointed out earlier, means lost resources to the domestic economy, and thus implies lost opportunities. It is paradoxical indeed that resources are flowing out of the developing countries rather than to them, where resources are most needed to finance growth and development. Even very poor countries have become net creditors to the rest of the world (see, e.g., Boyce & Ndikumana, 2001). Such lost resources do not contribute to the expansion of domestic economic activities and to improvement of the social welfare of domestic residents. Such lost resources, or more precisely, the accumulated lost resources, imply lost tax revenues. Given that developing countries face fiscal constraints, lost tax revenues imply foregone public goods, infrastructure and services, among others, essential to sustain growth. Or it can mean lost resources for debt servicing, contributing to worsening the social burden of external debts. Since institutions are generally weak, fragile or missing in the developing countries, the economic costs can be large and affect many in society. And because capital flight is often undertaken by the elite, the rest of society carries a disproportionate burden of the external debt. In fact, often the elite are able to shelter themselves from harm because they are able to move elsewhere and/or shelter their wealth abroad. Once again, from an economic justice point-of-view, there are distributive effects of external borrowing and capital flight that cannot be ignored.

In short, scholars are revisiting capital flight because of old and new issues. The lessons from the past remain relevant to the current context; but with new dimensions to the same problem, new lessons have to be learned as well. We hope that this article contributes to that end.

Before proceeding, there is one more issue that needs to be clarified, and that is the difference between normal capital flows and capital flight. First, we note that capital flight is a type of capital outflow but only because both have a feature in common – they are movements of capital across countries. But the similarity stops there. Capital flows represent portfolio decisions typically undertaken to exploit favourable returns to capital, among others. Capital flight, in contrast, represents a decision to take capital out and take refuge in another country to avoid social control.

Put another way, normal capital flows are like two-way streets in which the traffic of capital is dual-directional and presumably recorded in the official statistics (i.e., the balance of payments). In contrast, capital flight is more like a one-way street in which the traffic of capital is moving out and typically unrecorded. Sometimes capital flight is financed by capital inflows like external debts. At other times, capital flight itself finances the capital inflows, returning in the guise of foreign investments (often to take advantage of the incentives extended for overseas investors). In fact, it is possible to have large volumes of capital flow across countries and there is no capital flight involved. It is also possible to have no capital inflows to a country yet there are huge amounts of capital flight.

Lastly, we further note that when this capital flow perspective is employed, there will be a problem in understanding capital flight because the notion of optimal portfolio allocation precludes the consideration of unrecorded capital flows. Indeed, in two-way streets capital flows, there should not be any unrecorded capital flows, especially when the economic environment has been deregulated and financially liberalized. When there are unrecorded capital flows, they are to be considered integral and normal and, whatever their outcome, including adverse impacts on society, it is presumed to be an optimal situation. Clearly, such perspective ignores and does not see the social effects of capital flight, which can be significant and shouldered by the majority in society. Therefore, while both capital outflow and capital flight share a common feature, there are in fact unique characteristics to capital flight. As such, it may mean that countries take up policies that address capital flows but, at the same time, include policies that address capital flight itself.

**Theory**

In this article, we define 'capital flight' as the movement of capital from a resource-scarce developing country to avoid social control. 'Social control' means the actual or potential, as well as formal and informal, control on capital that includes, among others, taxation, regulation of the use of foreign exchange, the capacity to direct resources into productive activities, thus engendering growth, enhancing competitiveness, and consequently, realizing economic development.

We measure capital flight as the net unrecorded capital outflow or the residual between officially recorded sources and uses of funds. Recorded sources of funds are net additions to external debt (CDET) and net non-debt creating capital inflows (NKI). NKI is the sum of net direct foreign investments (FDI), net portfolio investment equities (PORT), and other investment assets (OTH). Recorded uses of funds are the current account deficits (CAD) and accumulation of international reserves (CRES) plus other official uses of foreign exchange sanctioned by the Central Bank. Note that 'net' means accounting all inflows and outflows of funds. Thus:

$$KF = CDET + NKI - CAD - CRES \qquad (1a)$$

which is called baseline capital flight (BKF). Positive BKF means capital flight; negative BKF means 'reverse' capital flight. Also, we follow the convention in the literature in which capital flight is denoted with a positive notation because capital flight is a form of accumulating foreign assets. 'Reverse' capital flight is like reducing foreign assets, thus a negative notation. Because the right hand side of Equation 1a contains variables that are considered officially recorded transactions, positive BKF therefore implies net unrecorded capital outflows and negative BKF, net unrecorded capital inflows.

The data used in the calculation have errors, so adjustments are needed to correct them. The first set of adjustments concerns the financial accounts. In particular, an adjustment is needed for the impact of exchange rate fluctuations on the stock of external debt (DEBT). Long-term external debts (LTDEBT) are normally denominated in a mix of hard currencies, and their fluctuations will affect the USD values of LTDEBT, which have implications for CDET. Thus the beginning-of-year adjusted external debt (ATTD) that accounts for foreign exchange rate fluctuations is:

$$ATTD_{-1} = \Sigma[(\alpha_{i,t-1}LTDEBT_{-1})(FX_i/FX_{i,-1})] + \Sigma\ (\beta_{i,-1}LTDEBT_{-1})$$
$$\phantom{ATTD_{-1} = }{}_{i=EU,\,UK,\,FF,\,DM,\,Yen,}\phantom{xxxxxxxxxxxxxxxxxx}{}_{SF\,i=USD,\,MULT,\,OTHER}$$

$$+ IMF_{-1}(SDR_t/SDR_{-1}) + STDEBT_{-1}, \tag{2}$$

where $\alpha_i$ is the proportion of LTDEBT in Euros (EU), £ sterling (UK), French francs (FF), German marks (DM), Japanese yens (Yen), and Swiss francs (SF); $\beta_i$ is the proportion of LTDEBT in USD, multiple and other currencies; FX is the exchange rate of the hard currencies to USD; IMF is use of IMF credits; SDR is the exchange rate between Special Drawing Rights and USD; STDEBT is short-term external debt.

The subscript $-1$ denotes the end of the last year (and hence, the beginning of the current year). Note that data for the currency composition of MULT, OTHER, and STDEBT are not available, and their dollar valuations are unadjusted. All things being equal, an appreciation in a hard currency relative to USD reduces $FX_i/FX_{i,-1}$ and $ATTD_{-1}$, so DEBT should be lower. With Equation 2, the adjustment factor for the impact of exchange rate fluctuations on the stock of external debt (ADEBT) is

$$ADEBT = ATTD_{-1} - DEBT_{-1}. \tag{3}$$

Equation 3 gives an estimate on the extent to which DEBT was affected by foreign exchange fluctuations. For instance, if the Japanese yen appreciated relative to USD, all things being equal, we expect to have a lower $ATTD_{-1}$ and ADEBT is negative. Thus CDET would not be an accurate estimate of the net inflow of new borrowing. Accordingly, we calculate the change in the adjusted external debt (CDET$_{ADJ}$).

Using Equation 3, we subtract ADEBT from CDET,

$$CDET_{ADJ} = CDET - ADEBT. \tag{4a}$$

Since $CDET = DEBT - DEBT_{-1}$, it can be shown that Equation 4a is equal to

$$CDET_{ADJ} = DEBT - ATTD_{-1}. \tag{4b}$$

Equation 1a can be re-calculated to obtain an adjusted baseline capital flight (KF$_{ADJ}$):

$$KF_{ADJ} = CDET_{ADJ} + NKI - CAD - CRES. \tag{1b}$$

Unfortunately, we are unable to calculate an adjustment for the discrepancies in direct foreign investments (FDI) and portfolio equities investments (PORT) because of data limitations. When data allows, the procedure would be similar to that of $CDET_{ADJ}$; that is, we obtain the discrepancies in the FDI data between source-country and host-country and calculate the impact of foreign exchange fluctuations. The same applies for PORT.

The second set of adjustments concerns the current account. In particular, an adjustment is needed to account for systematic trade misinvoicing, which can be measured via trading-partner data comparison. Import overinvoicing and export underinvoicing are often significant avenues for capital flight. Import under-invoicing (technical smuggling) is undertaken to evade customs duties and trade regulations, but conceptually, it is a form of 'reverse' capital flight in that it results in unrecorded flows of foreign exchange (smuggled goods must be paid for, even if they are not fully taxed). 'Pure' (as opposed to technical) smuggling in which imported goods are not taxed or recorded at all can be captured by trading partner data comparison. Export over-invoicing can happen if there are incentives on the export performance of industries that lead to invoice padding. In any of these cases, the current account is inaccurate, thus we need to make the adjustment.

To determine the magnitude of total trade mis-invoicing, we follow three steps. The first step is to compute the export mis-invoicing (DX) and import mis-invoicing (DM) for a country in its trade with major industrialized-country trading partners:

$$DX = PX - CIF*X, \tag{5a}$$

$$DM = M - CIF*PM, \tag{5b}$$

where PX is the industrialized-country trading-partner's imports from country i, and PM is the industrialized-country trading-partner's exports to country i; X and M are country i's exports to and imports from industrialized-country trading-partners, respectively; and CIF, the cif/fob factor, is an adjustment for the cost of freight and insurance. For Equations 5a and 5b, we utilize the trade data between country i and its industrialized-country trading-partners. The rationale for doing this is that the information from the industrialized countries is expected to be more reliable compared to the data from the developing countries. Accordingly, positive values of DX and DM indicate net export under-invoicing and net import over-invoicing, respectively; whereas negative values of DM and DM indicate net export over-invoicing and net import under-invoicing, respectively.

Next, we impute the global export and import trade discrepancies of country i (MISX and MISM, respectively). To obtain MISX and MISM, we multiply DX and DM by the reciprocal of the shares of all industrialized-country trading-partners to country i's total exports (X_INDUS) and total imports (M_INDUS):

$$MISX = DX/X\_INDUS, \tag{6a}$$

$$MISM = DM/M\_INDUS. \tag{6b}$$

The last step is to obtain total trade mis-invoicing (MIS) as the sum of Equations 6a and 6b. MIS is added to Equation 1b:

$$KF_{ADJ} = CDET_{ADJ} + NKI - CAD - CRES + MIS. \tag{1c}$$

In addition to the trade misinvoicing adjustment, we make another adjustment on the current account for the unrecorded income remittances (UNREMIT). For developing countries that have sizeable numbers of overseas workers, remittances are a significant component in the current account. If informal remittances are substantial, then it also requires an adjustment. To obtain an adjustment, we extrapolate the annual size of UNREMIT using an index for unrecorded remittance (UNREMIT Index):

$$UNREMIT = REMIT * UNREMIT \, Index, \tag{7}$$

where REMIT is recorded overseas remittances. UNREMIT is added to Equation 1c, thus

$$KF_{ADJ} = CDET_{ADJ} + NKI - CAD - CRES + MIS + UNREMIT, \tag{1d}$$

which is called total capital flight (TKF).

To make TKF figures comparable across periods, we calculate real capital flight (RKF), using the United States producer price index (PPI) in 1995 prices as the deflator:

$$RKF = TKF/PPI. \tag{8}$$

To make RKF comparable across countries, we determine the relative burden of RKF to the (size of the) economy; that is,

$$RKFGDP = RKF/RGDP, \tag{9}$$

where RKFGDP is the relative burden of RKF, and RGDP is real gross domestic product in 1995 prices.

Capital flight is (potentially, at least) capital invested abroad, so it will incur some returns. We compute the stock of capital flight (SKF) as

$$SKF = (1 + r)SKF_{-1} + TKF, \tag{10}$$

where r represents the 90-day United States Treasury Bill interest rate. Note that SKF is only an estimate of the total lost resources of country i, but it can be interpreted as a measure of the opportunity cost of capital flight.

## Hypotheses

In this article, we attempt to verify the following hypotheses. First, deregulation and financial liberalization increase both capital flight and external borrowing. That is to say, given the way economic reforms have been pursued in Indonesia, Malaysia, the Philippines, and Thailand, substantial amounts of the capital flows to these countries fuel capital flight; consequently, deregulation and financial liberalization did not bring about significant capital accumulation and financial deepening. Second, political and economic crises induce capital flight. In other words, capital flight is a response to increased risks in the domestic economy.

Putting together the two hypotheses, we can further hypothesize that because crises are more frequent and intense in post deregulation and financial liberalization periods, the magnitude of capital flight has risen and persistent as well. We will verify these hypotheses using descriptive-historical analysis.

## Analysis

We compiled the data from the following: IMF International Financial Statistics and Direction of Trade Statistics; and World Bank Global Development Finance and World Development Indicators. Given the nature of the reporting system for external debts and other data issues (see below), we utilize the World Bank's external debt data, specifically the Global Development Finance. Data for NKI, CAD, and CRES were taken from the Balance of Payments (summary statistics are available from the International Financial Statistics). For GDP, United States PPI, 90-day United States T-Bill interest rates, etc., we obtained data from the World Development Indicators. In addition, we visited the Bank Indonesia, the Bank Negara Malaysia, the Bangko Sentral ng Pilipinas, and the Bank of Thailand to discuss with the central bank staff our datasets and obtain updated information. Before proceeding to discuss the results, we deal with some data issues. Obviously, capital flight estimates differ because of variations in methodology and data. The main issue here is the following: What items comprise the officially recorded capital inflows and recorded foreign exchange outflows?

## External Debt

The first variable in the KF-equation concerns external debt, in particular, the additions to external debt (CDET). External debt information can be obtained from three sources: the OECD, the World Bank, and the IMF. The OECD utilizes what is called the creditor reporting system, while the World Bank uses the debtor reporting system (see, e.g., BIS-OECD-IMF-WB 1994). The IMF does not directly collect or report data on the stock of external debt but instead compiles the information from the OECD and WB. The Balance of Payments (BOP) accounts can be re-arranged to obtain the external debt flows, and by summing these flows over time, we get the stock of external debt. Provided that the coverage for DEBT is the same, both the OECD and the World Bank information complement each other.

The OECD and World Bank external debt data are stock figures, whilst the IMF data are flow figures. Chang *et al.* (1997) discuss issues concerning CDET when using figures from the World Bank as opposed to the IMF figures. They point out that CDET using the World Bank data are often larger than the flows reported in the IMF's data, and that this distinction is an indication that the World Bank data are relatively more complete and accurate than the IMF data.

There are also issues concerning the inclusion or exclusion or adjustment of the external debt data. The 'discovery' of old or existing external debt (say, during a rescheduling programme) will affect the World Bank's stock data but not the IMF flow data. In the World Bank procedure, the 'discovery' of debt is directly added to DEBT; but in the IMF procedure, it is not because the 'discovered' external debt is not a new debt inflow or disbursement. The World Bank revises its stock estimates for earlier years to incorporate this 'discovered' debt. For example, following the outbreak of the debt crises in 1983, debt stock data for the 1970s (published at the time in the World Bank's World Debt Tables) were extensively revised. In similar fashion, the 'discovery' of misreported external debts is subtracted from DEBT. As another example, the Bank of Thailand revised its external debt figures after finding in 2000 that DEBT was overstated by US$ 20 billion from 1995. Furthermore, adjustments on DEBT due to debt cancellations (or forgiveness) will reduce the stock figure. In the IMF's procedure, debt cancellations are reported like debt principal repayments (that is, a negative flow) with corresponding positive flows usually entered under the heading 'exceptional financing' in the BOP tables. Accordingly, given these issues, DEBT is the more accurate figure not only in terms of reflecting the current stock, but also in obtaining an accurate CDET.

Similar reasoning applies to the capitalization of interest arrears and the rescheduling or rollover of external debts and/or interest payments. The usual procedure is that interest payments due are reported in the BOP Table, with a counterpart entry made in the capital account. Because debt rescheduling and automatic rollover are not actual debt flows, flow data from the IMF may not reflect these changes. But they are recorded as an additional external debt in World Bank data.

The other main issue on DEBT is the following: what items should be included in a measure for external debt? Basically, there are two choices: 'gross' external debt or 'net' external debt. Gross external debt is the sum of all public external debts, (private) publicly guaranteed external debts, and private (not public guaranteed) debts. Net external debt is a narrower concept, which includes only public external debts and private publicly guaranteed external debts. In our view, gross external debt is more appropriate to use in capital flight measurement because all external borrowing generates inflows of foreign exchange regardless of whether the liability is public or private.

### Non-Debt Capital Flows

Net non-debt capital inflows (NKI) include net foreign direct investments (FDI), net portfolio equity investments (PORT), and other investment assets (OTH). A dual direction in foreign investments is to be expected when capital is mobile and economies are relatively open and integrated. Also, domestic residents and foreign residents can engage in foreign investments. OTH includes foreign currency deposits, which the banking and financial sectors hold as part of net open position (NOP). The liberalization of the financial account and financial sector meant that holding foreign currency deposits is now sanctioned by the central banks, especially as a way to cover for foreign exchange risks involving trade and/or corporate external debts. Note that the NOP includes only reported transactions. Note further that it is now possible for banks or financial institutions to place foreign exchange reserves abroad (as a form of investment) in order to gain some returns on capital (such activities are similar to portfolio investments), and the assumption here is that such transactions are recorded and reported in the

BOP, which may not be the case. Central banks can use swap facilities to manage foreign exchange risks and to cover for transaction costs in trade and/or payments for external debt, just like the private sector. Accordingly, NKI includes domestic residents' foreign investments and divestment abroad, as well as foreign residents' investments and divestment to the country

## Current Account

The current account (CA) is a major component of a country's officially recorded transactions with the rest of the world. The CA includes the trade balance (TB), meaning exports minus imports. In general, when TB is positive, or surplus, CA is also surplus; and vice versa. Thus often TB is used as proxy for CA. However, this interpretation may be misleading when a country has significant services transactions, which include interest payments, remittances, and other transfers. In particular, large interest payments can have serious implications on CA, and so CA is a better measure of non-financial account foreign exchange flows.

## International Reserves

Total international reserves (RES) refers to the total stock of foreign reserves and related assets. Accumulation of international reserves is CRES, which includes items like 'exceptional financing' which are counterpart entries for external debt adjustments such as cancellations. Other sanctioned uses of foreign exchange are also included in CRES, for example, private banks accumulation of reserves for trade financing.

## Discussion

Was capital fleeing South-east Asia? In this section, we discuss the results. Because of commonalities in endowments and economic structures, among others, we expect that Indonesia, Malaysia, the Philippines, and Thailand have similar issues linked to capital flight. For instance, the four countries have external debt problems, though the level of indebtedness differs among them (see Table 1). Likewise, each has pursued deregulation and financial liberalization programmes, experienced massive capital flows, especially during the 1990s, and recently, had financial and economic crises. But they have unique characteristics and development experiences such as differences in how economic reforms have been pursued or implemented in each country.

## Indonesia

### *Garuda Capital*[1]

Total capital flight (TKF) from Indonesia was increasing from the 1970s to the late 1990s, but declined after 1999. In fact, TKF was negative in 2002. Note that in Figure 1 TKF followed a secular break in its trend; that is, the 1970s had a particular level, then another one for the 1980s to the mid 1990s. This pattern can be the result of deregulation and financial liberalization programmes that began in the mid-1980s. In our calculations, TKF for the 1970s was US$ 26 billion. For the 1980s, it was US$ 66 billion; for the 1990s, US$ 123 billion. In the early 2000s, TKF was US$ 12 billion. Thus, between 1970 and 2002, TKF was US$ 228 billion. We calculated the stock of capital flight (SKF) at US$ 365 billion as of 2002. These figures mean that Indonesia lost significant amounts of resources to capital flight.

In Figure 2, we show TKF as a share of gross domestic product (GDP). The trend is similar to that in Figure 1, except that the former reveals more pronounced peaks of TKF in the mid-1980s and late 1990s. These spikes, and also that in the mid 1970s, are associated with economic and political crises in the country that made capital flee.

Considering that Indonesia achieved an impressive and fairly stable economic performance in three decades since the 1970s, despite experiencing some crises along the way, we think that trends in the country's economic growth may not be able to explain the swings in capital flight. As Figure 2 shows, Indonesia sustained its economic expansion except in two periods under the New Order: 1982 and 1998–99. In fact, only in 1975, the latter part of the 1980s, 1991, and the late 1990s did capital flight exceed economic growth rates, which again are crises years. In 1975, Indonesia experienced a debt-related crisis, when the government-owned oil company, Pertamina, defaulted on its US$ 10 billion external debt (about US$ 4 billion was short term debt). In the late 1980s, the fall in global commodity prices (especially, oil) and a BOP crisis led to a slowdown in economic growth but was quickly addressed by the government with the introduction of reform programmes. In the early 1990s, Indonesia had banking mini-crises in 1990–91 and 1993–94, a stock market crash in 1991, and a speculative attack on the rupiah in 1994. In the late 1990s, there was the 1997–98 Asian Crisis and a political implosion that led to President Mohamed Suharto's resignation. Also, Suharto's health and doubts about his political leadership became important issues after 1995. But, in the earlier crises before 1998, Indonesia was able to recover quickly and regain growth because the government

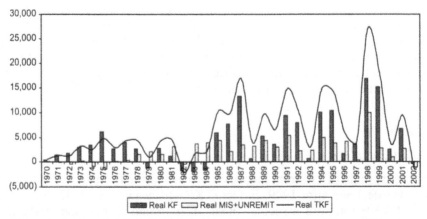

**Figure 1.** Total capital flight from Indonesia, 1970–2002 (US$ millions; 1995 prices)

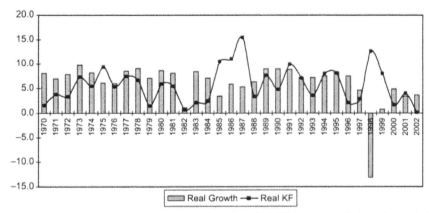

**Figure 2.** Economic growth rates and share of total capital flight to GDP, Indonesia 1970–2002 (1995 prices)

was ready to implement monetary and fiscal restraints to control inflation and stabilize the economy. Nonetheless, the swings in capital flight appear to be linked to weak financial governance (e.g., absent legal reforms on bankruptcy and bank supervision) and political uncertainties in the country. As Figure 2 indicates, most of the large swings in capital flight occurred after the mid-1980s when banking deregulation was implemented. Also, by the late 1990s, doubts about Suharto's commitment to pursue the needed reform programmes were crucial in undermining confidence in the country's stability and economic growth. In addition, there was no known successor to the Presidency. When Suharto's leadership collapsed in 1998, aggravated by social unrest, there was panic and massive capital flight. Although a degree of economic stability has returned, there remained political uncertainty in the 2000s. But very little capital inflow has taken place since 1998. As such, there has been a downward trend in capital flight.

## Malaysia

### Capital Flight Boleh[2]

Malaysia had very high total capital flight (TKF), especially in the 1990s. Note in Figure 3, TKF was relatively stable in the 1970s to the 1980s. But, in the 1990s, TKF increased significantly. Apart from 1997 to 1998, when TKF dropped to low levels, the trend has remained high but stable from the mid 1990s. We calculated TKF in the 1970s at US$ 21 billion. In the 1980s it was US$ 27 billion; and in the 1990s, US$ 98 billion. In the early 2000s, TKF was US$ 46 billion. In the period 1970 to 2002, TKF reached US$ 192 billion. The stock of capital flight (SKF) was US$ 290 billion as of 2002. Clearly, Malaysia lost significant amounts of resources to capital flight.

Figure 4 presents TKF in shares of gross domestic product (GDP). Interestingly, the trend reveals some peaks in 1974, 1977, 1987, 1994, and also falls in 1988 and 1998. These years appear to coincide with the 11 to 12 year business cycle of the Malaysia economy. The trend since 1999 is also interesting in that TKF remained

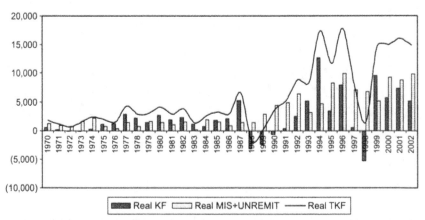

**Figure 3.** Total capital flight, Malaysia 1970–2002 (US$ millions; 1995 prices)

high but relatively stable. Also, Figure 4 shows a break in the trend around the late 1980s.

Furthermore, Figure 4 indicates that the peaks can be linked to the economic crises in Malaysia, in particular, a recession in the mid-1970s, the Industrial Coordination Act (ICA), the banking and political crises in the late 1980s, and the 1997–98 Asian Crisis. In the latter two cases, we found that the total swing in TKF was at least 15 per cent of GDP. But interestingly, except in 1974, the mid-1980s, 1998, and 2001, economic growth rates remained high, even with capital flight.

We again highlight institutional factors to explain capital flight. Because the domestic economy is small, Malaysia needed to adjust to external factors. Arguably, domestic factors are more important in explaining trends in TKF. So for instance, the National Economic Policy (NEP) and its associated programmes are key factors in considering capital flight in the 1970s and the 1980s. While it can be argued that the NEP was achieving its targets, the peaks in the latter part of the

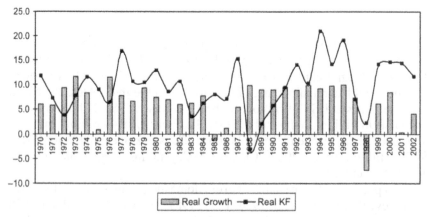

**Figure 4.** Economic growth rates and share of total capital flight to GDP, Malaysia 1970– 2002 (1995 prices)

1980s can be in part because of concerns of a repeat of the 1969 ethnic riots. Also economic and political leadership crises contributed to the uncertainties both in the late 1980s and late 1990s.

In addition, the succession of political and economic scandals in the early 1980s, then an economic recession in the mid 1980s, are all important factors to explain why during that period (in fact, since 1975) capital flight remained high. By the late 1980s, there was negative capital flight, perhaps reflecting the impact of wide-scale privatization of government-owned enterprises. We note that it is possible that some of the capital inflows at this time were repatriated capital flight. We further note that the 1987–88 Malaysian banking crisis led to the introduction of stricter measures for bank surveillance and regulation, so arguably, there was enhanced financial governance by the 1990s.

But the application of capital controls in 1994 was perceived by investors as a reversal of the deregulation and financial liberalization programs, which partly explain the surge of capital flight. There was again a surge in 1996, which can be due to the surge in capital inflows to Malaysia. Yet the second application of capital controls in 1998 was considered effective in reducing capital flight, although it can be argued that the 1998 controls were too late so perhaps capital that wanted to leave had already left when the policy was implemented. Interestingly enough, when the controls were lifted in 1999, there was a surge in capital flight. Throughout this period, Prime Minister Mahathir Mohammad provided leadership for government intervention, thus insulating Malaysia from the adverse impacts of the crises and capital flight.

## The Philippines

### Capital Flight 2000[3]

In Figure 5, we find that total capital flight (TKF) from the Philippines followed a cyclical pattern from 1970 until mid-1990s. Arguably, this pattern reflects the economic boom-bust cycle that the country experienced throughout in the post-World War II period. In the post-Marcos period, there was optimism that the

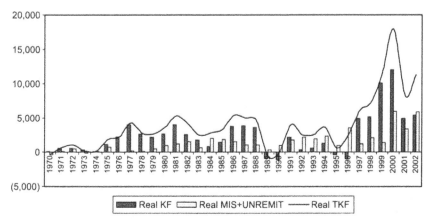

**Figure 5.** Total capital flight, the Philippines 1970–2002 (US$ millions; 1995 prices)

Philippines will finally achieve an economic take off. But the combination of policy failures, political instability, and natural calamities postponed economic takeoff and the country regressed back to boom-bust cycle. So what appears to be a different trend in the early 1990s is actually part of the overall boom–bust cycle. From the mid-1990s, the trend indicated a rapid rise in TKF and remained high since 2000s. We argue that this finding is consistent with the economic–capital– flight boom–bust cycle of the Philippines; that is, during an economic bust, TKF was in a boom, and the TKF cycle tapers off in the latter stage of a crisis when most of the capital had left. The reverse pattern applies when the Philippines was in an economic boom.

The frequency of the TKF cycle is consistent with the Philippines recent economic history in which the economic boom often spans a brief period (usually three to four years) often cut abruptly by an external or internal crisis. The pattern since the mid-1990s was perhaps driven by deregulation and financial liberalization and the return of foreign capital to the country. Total TKF in the 1970s was US$ 16 billion. For the 1980s, it was US$ 36 billion; for the 1990s, US$ 48 billion. In the early 2000s, TKF was US$ 37 billion. For the whole period, we estimated TKF at US$ 138 billion. The stock of capital flight (SKF) was US$ 218 billion as of 2002. Thus the Philippines lost significant amounts of resources to capital flight in the last three decades.

In Figure 6 we find that high levels of capital flight occurred during periods of domestic economic crises, especially in the 1980s to the early 1990s. In the early 1980s, the Latin American debt crisis was an important trigger of the 1983–84 Balance of Payments crises in the Philippines. In the years before the crises, the country was already experiencing a rapid slowdown in economic growth as debt burden and global economic slowdown took their toll on the economy. The assassination of President Ferdinand Marcos' political arch rival, Senator Benigno Aquino, in 1983 and the ensuing political and social unrest aggravated the economic uncertainty. The final blow was the deep recession in 1984–85. Thus we can see substantial flight of capital in the first half of the 1980s until 1988.

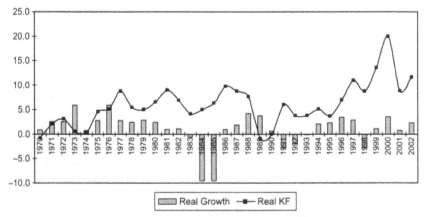

**Figure 6.** Economic growth rates and share of total capital flight to GDP, the Philippines 1970–2002 (1995 prices)

In 1986, Corazon Aquino was installed as President. But the following years were difficult. A series of coups d'état from 1986 to 1989 undermined economic and political stability, and a recession and an electricity power supply crisis in 1991 to 1992 stalled any economic recovery. From 1993, the Philippines appeared to be on track for an economic turnaround, experiencing its longest economic expansion since the mid 1980s, but with the 1997–98 Asian Crisis, economic recovery was again interrupted. As in the previous decades, economic slowdown appears to have resulted in flight of capital. Fortunately, because the Philippines had a shorter period for capital accumulation, flight of capital in the late 1990s was not as great as in the other affected countries in the region.

After 1998, concerns about the domestic economy re-emerged, especially after the election of Joseph Estrada to the presidency. What happened in the late 1990s seems similar to the early decades: domestic economic and political instability induced capital flight. Estrada's impeachment in 2000, social unrest in 2001, and the insecurity of the successor government of President Macapagal-Arroyo reinforced doubts of the country's ability to sustain economic growth. We thus find that since 1998, capital flight has been considerable and generally rising. What is particularly interesting in Figure 6 is the peak in 2000, which perhaps reflects how political factors impact on a highly liberalized but weak economy.

## Thailand

### *Sawasdee Capital*[4]

Up to the mid-1990s, total capital flight (TKF) from Thailand was relatively low. Only in the late 1990s did it reach extraordinary levels. In Figure 7, we show trends in TKF for the whole period. Like the Philippines, the trend indicates that Thailand's TKF followed a cyclical pattern, which was very pronounced in the late 1980s, early 1990s, and late 1990s. Democracy and sound macroeconomic policies characterized the economic boom that began in the late 1980s, which coincided with the end of Prime Minister Prem Tinsulanonda's regime in 1988. Thus the two upsurges in the late 1980s and late 1990s can be due to the banking

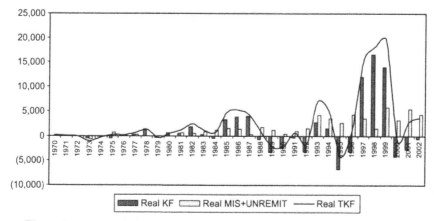

**Figure 7.** Total Capital Flight, Thailand 1970-2002 (USD millions; 1995 prices)

and economic crises, whilst that of the early 1990s can be due to political crises (e.g., the coup d'état in 1992). We calculated TKF in the 1970s at US$ 0.9 billion. For the 1980s, it jumped to US$ 20 billion. For the 1990s, TKF was US$ 70 billion. In the early 2000s, TKF was US$ 8 billion. For the whole period, TKF was US$ 100 billion. The stock of capital flight (SKF) was US$ 136 billion in 2002. Like its neighbours, Thailand lost a significant amount of resources to capital flight. But among the four countries, it had the least capital flight.

Figure 8 presents TKF in shares of gross domestic product (GDP). Thailand had two periods when capital flight was significant: in the late 1980s and in the late 1990s. Both periods refer to Thailand's two banking crises. But the figure shows that economic growth rates continued to increase after the first banking crisis in the mid-1980s, while capital flight decreased. Before 1985, high economic growth was likewise associated with lower capital flight. But the second banking crisis resulted in a deep recession and thus high capital flight. It is important to note that prior to the 1990s, bank regulations and controls were consistently undermined by the economic and political elite, who were more interested in enhancing their wealth and power (see, e.g., Apichat, 2002). In addition, capital flows were greatly facilitated by deregulation and financial liberalization, especially with the creation of the Bangkok International Banking Facility (BIBF) in 1993.

Despite robust economic growth rates, macroeconomic indicators started to reveal some fundamental weaknesses in the economy, yet no adjustments were made. For instance, the Thai baht remained overvalued and pegged to the US dollar. In the mid-1990s, the real estate sector was in excess supply. Also important, the economy was overexposed to short-term external debt, and its external sector was weak, experiencing a sudden drop from a 2-digit growth rate in exports the previous years to − 1 per cent in 1996. Also, there were speculative attacks on the Thai baht in 1996. But even with these signals, the Thai government remained indecisive in responding with the required policy reforms and macroeconomic adjustment programmes. Thus when the Asian crisis exploded in 1997, massive capital flight was not a surprise, and it continued

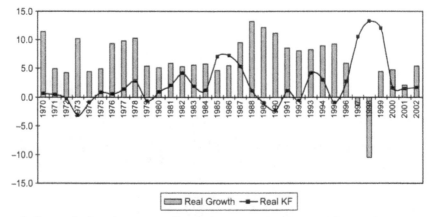

**Figure 8.** Economic Growth Rates and Share of Total Capital Flight to GDP, Thailand 1970-2002 (1995 prices)

into the late 1990s. In fact, capital flight started a little earlier before the beginning of the crisis. By 2000, most of the liquid capital had already left. While there has been a strong recovery since 1999, concerns about weak financial governance remains, while the level of capital inflow to Thailand had not returned to pre-crisis levels, at least by 2002.

## Implications for Theory and Policy

We have demonstrated that large amounts of resources from Southeast Asia were lost to capital flight. To Indonesia, Malaysia, the Philippines, and Thailand, capital flight means significant lost opportunities, and by extension, significant externalities. Given the large unaccounted impact of capital flight to the four countries, we therefore argue that government action is necessary and should be required to address the problem. Secondly, because the upsurge in capital flight coincided with deregulation and financial liberalization, we question conventional wisdom that when such policies are implemented, there would be no more capital flight; that is, free access to, and movement of, international capital will encourage businesses, create more jobs, and build productive infrastructures in the domestic economy. In fact, given our findings from the four countries, deregulation and financial liberalization facilitated inflows of foreign savings but these were increasingly used to fuel capital flight. In other words, more opportunities for capital flight are available today. As the four countries implemented deregulation and financial liberalization programmes, they should have introduced and strengthened the financial regulatory mechanisms and processes to control capital flight. Given that economic and political crises and shocks reinforced flight, we challenge the governments of these countries to secure economic and political stability in order to provide conditions that engender economic expansion and development.

More specific to capital flight, the large amounts of capital flight imply the need to have capital management techniques and related policies in place to keep resources in the domestic economy (see also Crotty & Epstein, 1999; Epstein *et al.*, 2003). The fact that capital flight implies lost opportunities also means that there are unaccounted adverse effects on society (i.e., externalities), and therefore government intervention is necessary and indeed justified. The government then must explore alternative ways to regulate capital flows and control capital flight. The objective is not to return to or impose financial repression. Rather, the goal is for the governments to regain control over macroeconomic policies and the direction of economic growth and development. For example, capital controls can be used to affect both the volume and composition of capital formation, especially in directing funds to the tradable or productive sectors in order to push the country to sustainable industrialization. Indeed, given deregulation and financial liberalization, and their concomitant processes, the institutions for governance have to be put in place and administrative capacity has to be strengthened in order for reforms to bring about their intended outcome. What this requires is a reorientation of points-of-view on the part of government in the economy; that is, a rethinking of what government intervention means in the present economic realities.

## Implications for Management And/or Business

Given the experiences of Indonesia, Malaysia, the Philippines, and Thailand we discuss implications for management to address capital flows in the region and, in particular, capital flight. The first issue concerns macroeconomic performance. The point is that with sound policy management, monetary and fiscal programmes engender economic growth. A sound management of the macro economy is therefore needed. Thus unsustainable current and budget deficits, unsound foreign exchange rates, unstable inflation, and interest rates that will discourage investments remain important concerns. But whatever policy combination is pursued by the government, the end goal is an expansion of sustainable production to increase incomes and provide more opportunities to people. Policies that are based on compromises are not helpful at all. We contend that in the cases of Indonesia, Malaysia, the Philippines, and Thailand, economic growth and employment generation must have equal weight on the economic management agenda. Both objectives can be pursued together.

Second, for the four countries, it is important to strengthen their macro-organizational fundamentals; that is, policies to strengthen the institutional capacity of the government covering, among others, financial governance and administrative capacity. It entails the development of the countries' financial sector, in particular, deepening banking and capital markets. It is important to have financial systems that are able to mobilize domestic savings and capital markets that facilitate the transfers of internal and external savings and lead to capital accumulation. It is important to have a robust real sector that produces goods and services both for the domestic and global markets. So macro-organizational fundamentals mean production that is progressively upgraded on the industrial ladder; that is, pursuing technological adoption and adaptation and reducing reliance on imported inputs and capital goods.

It goes without saying that the above points complement each other. To facilitate this process, we propose to bring back the government to centre stage in public policy. In their management of the macro economy, the governments of Indonesia, Malaysia, the Philippines, and Thailand must emphasize domestic responsibility, especially in setting economic goals and articulating a vision of economic development. The governments must choose policies that reflect domestic characteristics and contexts (e.g. choosing an appropriate monetary policy to encourage domestic investments). In addition, governments must be embedded in society to be able to respond to domestic challenges, including the provision of social safety nets, yet autonomous so it can withstand external challenges. Moreover, the governments must curb economic and social processes that are counter-productive to realizing robust macroeconomic performance and maintaining the macro-organizational fundamentals (e.g., putting restraints on speculative capital flows, managing external borrowing, and monitoring economic activities, especially the unproductive ones.). In addition, the governments must promote and enable relationships to realize macroeconomic and macro-organizational goals (e.g. enabling and allowing government–business cooperation and more meaningful participation by civil society).

There is also a need to have effective economic management at international level. In particular, increased global financial integration has demonstrated that what could be a minor financial shock can snowball into a major financial crisis in another country or region. At the same time, globalization in trade means that production across countries is now inter-connected. Accordingly, the international community must take up responsibility and pursue actions to discipline or regulate activities within their national borders before unfavourable developments occur elsewhere. The 1997–98 Asian Crisis, in part the result of financial globalization, raised the need for management coordination so that capital surges, for example, will not again cause havoc in other places. In the event of an economic or financial crisis, it is important that the international community take up the challenge to contribute to economic recovery and rehabilitation efforts in the affected countries.

Finally, we have a strong argument for a better management of external debts by debtors and creditors alike. Debtor countries are responsible for making sure that external debts benefit the majority in society and not used to enrich a few. Thus a government that misuses funds is itself liable for the external debt and should not impose the burden on the public. Similarly, creditors share responsibility in the prudent management of external debts. Such a role can be achieved either through an application of sound lending policy or some form of involvement in the effective use or disbursement of funds. In some cases, where external borrowings have been actually misused, or proof cannot be presented to demonstrate that the funds were actually used to improve the social conditions of domestic residents, or the borrowed funds cannot be traced, we can conclude that the funds were diverted to private pockets, and more likely as capital flight. If creditors ignore or pretend not to see that the borrowed funds were being used to benefit only a few, or they do not act to redress the situation, they likewise are accountable for the indebtedness of developing countries. In such cases, we have to question the legitimacy of the external debt itself and the rationale for continuing to honour such debts that society on the whole did not benefit from. Accordingly, some debt relief should be demanded from the creditors so that developing countries will not continue to bear the consequences of the greed of a few.

## Conclusions

Was capital fleeing South-east Asia? Using a procedure to estimate capital flight, we can conclude that Indonesia, Malaysia, the Philippines, and Thailand experienced substantial capital flight over the period 1970 to 2002. As expected, capital flight was high during periods of crises. What was interesting is that there were cases when capital flight was also high during periods of robust economic growth. What was also interesting is that capital flight increased in the period of deregulation and financial liberalization.

In summary, total capital flight from Indonesia was estimated at US$ 228 billion. For Malaysia, we estimated total capital flight at US$ 192 billion. The Philippines had US$ 138 billion, and Thailand had US$ 100 billion. Aggregating the figures from the four countries, we obtain US$ 658 billion. Counting imputed interest rate earnings on capital flight over the three decades, we obtain a total of US$ 1 trillion as of 2002, of which US$ 365 billion was for Indonesia, US$ 290 billion for Malaysia, US\$ 218 billion for the Philippines, and US\$ 136 billion for Thailand. Indeed, these are significant amounts of lost resources that could have been used in the domestic economy to generate more output, create additional jobs, thus producing a better quality of economic growth, and in the end, realizing higher social welfare in the countries.

Finally, to address capital flight, we argued that some policies need to be in place. For instance, governments must pursue policies that will strengthen the macroeconomic performance and macro-organizational fundamentals. It is important that governments are embedded in their societies and promote domestic responsibility in setting economic targets and articulating a vision of economic development, especially not ignoring the domestic characteristics and contexts. At the same time, the international community has to contribute to this endeavour as well. Governments must also institute some form of capital management techniques to retain capital in the domestic economy, direct resources into productive uses, and thus reduce capital flight. Lastly, there is a need for better management of external debts by debtors and creditors alike. Arguably, these are lofty guidelines, to say the least. But, as we expounded in the cases of Indonesia, Malaysia, the Philippines, and Thailand, the stakes involved with capital flight in these countries are likewise very high.

## Acknowledgements

We thank Germelino Bautista, James K. Boyce, Gerald Epstein, Jomo K.S., the staff at the Bank Indonesia, the Bank Negara Malaysia, the Bangko Sentral ng Pilipinas, the Bank of Thailand, the Southeast Asia Central Banks Research and Training Centre, and the two anonymous referees for comments. Funding for this research was provided by the Political Economy Research Institute, the Social Science Research Council, the John D. and Catherine T. MacArthur Foundation, and the Helenica Foundation. The author is currently based at the United Nations Development Programme, Asia and the Pacific Regional Center. The usual disclaimer applies.

## Notes

[1] In the mythology of the Ramayana, Shiva, the god of preservation, descends to Earth riding the mystical bird, Garuda. Adapting this mythology to capital flight, we claim that capital enters Indonesia 'riding' the Garuda and preserves the country. But there also lies the paradox of capital: once capital falls off the Garuda, Indonesia experiences an economic crisis. Hence we say 'Garuda Capital Flight'.

[2] 'Boleh' means 'can do'. 'Malaysia boleh!' or 'Malaysia can do it!' was a slogan used by Mahathir to galvanize Malaysians to pursue higher economic goals. Hence the response to economic vision of Malaysia 2020 (i.e., attain developed country status by 2020) would be 'Malaysia boleh!' Behind this vision is the notion that Malaysia is a relatively strong economy with sound financial structures and therefore capital will remain in the country. But there lies the paradox: while the financial system is indeed well regulated, the other sectors are not. Hence we say: 'Capital Flight Boleh!'

[3] To transform the Philippines from its dismal status as the 'sick man' of Asia, Fidel Ramos embarked on an economic programme to make the country take off to NIC-hood at the turn of the 21st century. Thus the slogan: 'Philippines 2000!' From 1992, massive and rapid deregulation and liberation programmes were undertaken but without instituting or neglecting the requisite governance reforms. We adapt the Ramos slogan. Hence we say: 'Capital Flight 2000!'

[4] In Thai, '*sawasdee*' means 'hello' or 'goodbye,' which is typically uttered only once during the day. That is, when one meets a friend for the first time during the day, one greets the other by saying '*sawasdee*' (of course, conjugated according to gender); when one leaves and it is definite that one will not see the other for the day, one says '*sawasdee*' as well. Here, we adapt this expression to capital entering Thailand. Hence we say '*sawasdee* capital'. With capital leaving Thailand for good in a crisis, we also say '*sawasdee* capital'.

# References

Apichat Satitniramai (2002) The Rise and Fall of the Technocrats: Unholy Trinity of Technocrats, Ruling Elites and Private Bankers and Genesis of the 1997 Economic Crisis unpublished Ph.D. dissertation, University of Wales, Swansea.

Bank of International Settlements–International Monetary Fund–Organization of Economic Cooperation and Development–World Bank [BIS–IMF–OECD–WB] (1994) *Debt Stocks, Debt Flows and the Balance of Payments* (Basle, Switzerland: Bank of International Settlements–International Monetary Fund–Organization of Economic Cooperation and Development–World Bank).

Beja, Jr. E. (2005) External Borrowing and Capital Flows: Revisiting the 'Revolving Door' Model of Capital Flight, paper presented at the Ateneo Center for Asian Studies Conference on *Globalization and Nationalism in the Asian Context*, Manila, 12 Aug.

Boyce, J. K. (1992) The revolving door? external debt and capital flight: a Philippine case study, *World Development*, 20(3), pp. 335–349.

Boyce, J. K. & Ndikumana, L. (2001) Is Africa a net debtor? New estimates of capital flight from severely indebted sub-Saharan African countries, 1970–98, *Journal of Development Studies*, 38(2), pp. 27–56.

Chang, K., Claessens Stijn & Cumby, R. (1997) Conceptual and methodological issues in the measurement of capital flight, *International Journal of Financial Economics*, 2, pp. 101–119.

Collier, P., Hoeffler, A. & Patillo, C. (2004) Africa's exodus: capital flight and the brain drain as portfolio decisions, *Journal of African Economies*, 13, pp. 15–54.

Crotty, J. & Epstein, G. (1999) In defense of capital controls in light of the Asian financial crisis, *Journal of Economic Issues*, 33(2), pp. 427–433.

Eichengreen, B. & Mussa, M. (1998) Capital account liberalization: theoretical and empirical aspects, International Monetary Fund, *Occasional Papers* No 172.

Epstein, G., Grabel, I. & Jomo, K. S. (2003) Capital management techniques in developing countries, Political Economy Research Institute, *Working Paper* No 56.

Furman, A. & Stiglitz, J. (1998) Economic crisis and insights from East Asia, *Brookings Papers on Economic Activity*, 2, pp. 1–135.

Gibson, H. & Tskalotos, E. (1993) Testing a flow model of capital flight in five European countries, *Manchester School*, 61(2), pp. 141–166.

Griffith-Jones, S., Gottschalk, R. & Cailloux, J. (2003) *International Capital Flows in Calm and Turbulent Times* (Ann Arbor: University of Michigan Press).

Helleiner, E. (1994) *States and the Reemergence of Global Finance: From Bretton Woods to the 1990s* (Ithaca: Cornell University Press).

Kindleberger, C. (1987) A Historical Perspective, in: D. Lessard & J. Williamson (Eds) *Capital Flight and Third World Debt*, pp. 7–28 (Washington, DC: Institute of International Economics).

Lessard, D. & Williamson, J. (1987) *Capital Flight and the Third World Debt* (Washington, DC: Institute of International Economics).

Leung, Hing-Man (2003) External Debt & Worsening Business Cycles in Less Developed Countries, *Journal of Economic Studies*, 30(2), pp. 155–168.

Palma, G. (2003) The Three Routes to Financial Crises: Chile, Mexico and Argentina [1], Brazil [2]; and Korea, Malaysia and Thailand [3], in: H.-J. Chang (Ed.) *Rethinking Development Economics*, pp. 347–376 (London: Anthem Press).

Prasad, E., Rogoff, R., Shang-Jin Wei & Kose, M. A. (2003) The Effects of Financial Globalization on Developing Countries: Some Empirical Evidence, National Bureau of Economic Research, Working Paper 10492.

World Bank (1993) *The East Asian Miracle: Economic Growth and Public Policy* (New York: Oxford University Press).

# How Do the Asian Economies Compete With Japan in the US Market? Is China Exceptional? A Triangular Trade Approach

YUSHI YOSHIDA & HIRO ITO

## Introduction

For China, unquestionably, the US and Japan are the most important trading partners besides Hong Kong, and their importance is increasing especially for the recent years. Before China started liberalizing its economy, Hong Kong played the important role as a middleman between China and the rest of the world (see Fung and Iizaka, 1998); in 1992, Hong Kong was China's biggest trading partner in both exports and imports (in terms of traded values; see Table 1). In recent years, with its economic liberalization efforts, China started trading more directly with the rest of the world while Hong Kong's role as a middleman has dwindled. Nonetheless, if we assume the indirect trade that flows via Hong Kong to China is proportional to the direct trade flows to China, we could say that the US and Japan have been the two largest trading partners in both exports and imports during the last decade. Between 1992 and 2000, China's imports from Japan tripled from $13.7 billion to $41.5 billion while the imports from the US more than doubled from $8.9 billion to $22.4 billion (Table 1). During the same period, China's

**Table 1.** China's trade with major trading partners

(thousands of dollars)

Imports

| | 1992 | | 1995 | | 1998 | | 2000 | |
|---|---|---|---|---|---|---|---|---|
| 1. | Hong Kong | 20,533,589 | Japan | 29,004,529 | Japan | 28,275,074 | Japan | 41,509,675 |
| 2. | Japan | 13,682,461 | US | 16,118,291 | US | 16,883,171 | Taiwan | 25,493,561 |
| 3. | US | 8,900,735 | Taiwan | 14,783,944 | Taiwan | 16,631,051 | Korea | 23,207,406 |
| 4. | Taiwan | 5,865,971 | Korea | 10,293,234 | Korea | 15,014,348 | US | 22,363,148 |
| 5. | Germany | 4,015,042 | Hong Kong | 8,590,713 | Germany | 7,020,657 | Germany | 10,408,731 |
| | World | 80,585,333 | World | 132,083,539 | World | 140,236,807 | World | 225,093,731 |

Exports

| | 1992 | | 1995 | | 1998 | | 2000 | |
|---|---|---|---|---|---|---|---|---|
| 1. | Hong Kong | 37,512,229 | Hong Kong | 35,983,427 | Hong Kong | 38,741,792 | US | 52,099,220 |
| 2. | Japan | 11,678,713 | Japan | 28,466,685 | US | 37,947,666 | Hong Kong | 44,518,285 |
| 3. | US | 8,593,800 | US | 24,713,498 | Japan | 29,660,114 | Japan | 41,654,314 |
| 4. | Germany | 2,447,990 | Korea | 6,687,805 | Germany | 7,354,309 | Korea | 11,292,364 |
| 5. | Korea | 2,404,912 | Germany | 5,671,451 | Korea | 6,251,516 | Germany | 9,277,790 |
| | World | 84,940,062 | World | 148,779,565 | World | 183,809,065 | World | 249,202,551 |

*Source*: ITCS, OECD

exports to Japan increased almost four-fold from $11.7 billion to $41.6 billion, and its exports to the US rose more than six-fold from $8.6 billion to $52.1 billion.

In this study, we investigate the dynamics of the trilateral trade relationship between China, Japan and the US. In what we call the 'triangular trade approach,' we explore how Japanese trade with and foreign direct investment in China affect Chinese exports to the US market. Moreover, in order to shed light on the possible peculiarity of Chinese trade, we apply the trilateral trade approach to seven other East Asian countries and examine the effect of Japanese trade and foreign direct investment (FDI) on these countries' exports to the USA. For the reminder of the article, we refer to these countries and China as 'third countries' for convenience.

In the triangular trade approach, we regress the exports of the third countries to the US on the Japanese exports to the US as well as those to the third countries in a panel data specification while controlling for Japanese FDI and other macroeconomic variables. With this approach, we can reveal whether Japanese exports to the USA and those to China (or other third countries) are substitutes or complements. By incorporating Japanese firms' FDI activities, we can also examine if Japanese multinational corporations are shifting their production bases to China (or other third countries in East Asia) and how that affects the exports from China (or other third countries) to the USA.

One of this study's contributions is that we examine bilateral trade flows in a three-country framework. Most of the past empirical works on international trade consider bilateral trade in a two-country framework. However, we think that empirical studies with a two-country framework, most notably gravity models, ignore an important trade determinant, that is, the influence of a third country's trade flows.

Our main empirical results are as follows. First, we find that Japanese exports to China seem to promote Chinese exports to the USA. However, after controlling for Japan's FDI to China, the trade enhancing effect of Japanese exports disappears, indicating that Chinese exports to the US are promoted partly by Japanese companies' efforts to shift their production bases to China. We do not find this relationship in other East Asian countries. Second, when controlling for the US market size for each commodity, we find that the exports from some of our sample Asian countries and Japanese exports are competing in the US market. However, the degree of the competition is higher for China than other Asian countries.

## Economic Linkage Between Asian Economies: The Trade-FDI Nexus

As has been well-documented, the USA and Japan have been the most important trading partners for the East Asian economies for decades. Table 2 presents the shares of Japan and the US in the trade of the East Asian countries between 1990 and 2000. The table shows that the USA has been an important destination for Asian exports while Japan is an important exporter to these countries. The share of the USA as the export destination ranges from 14 per cent (Indonesia) to 30 per cent (Philippines), while that of Japan as the import source country varies from 16 per cent (Indonesia) to 25 per cent (Thailand). From these data, we can make a generalization that Japan exports to East Asia while the latter exports to the USA.

**Table 2.** Shares of trade with Japan and the US among the Asian countries

Exporting Country

| | 1990 | | 1995 | | 2000 | |
|---|---|---|---|---|---|---|
| | Japan | US | Japan | US | Japan | US |
| China | 0.15 | 0.08 | 0.19 | 0.17 | 0.17 | 0.21 |
| Korea | 0.19 | 0.29 | 0.13 | 0.19 | 0.12 | 0.22 |
| Hong Kong | 0.06 | 0.24 | 0.06 | 0.22 | 0.06 | 0.23 |
| Singapore | 0.09 | 0.21 | 0.08 | 0.18 | 0.08 | 0.17 |
| Thailand | 0.17 | 0.23 | 0.17 | 0.18 | 0.15 | 0.21 |
| Indonesia | 0.43 | 0.13 | 0.27 | 0.14 | 0.23 | 0.14 |
| Philippine | 0.20 | 0.38 | 0.16 | 0.36 | 0.15 | 0.30 |
| Malaysia | 0.15 | 0.17 | 0.12 | 0.21 | 0.13 | 0.21 |

Importing Country

| | 1990 | | 1995 | | 2000 | |
|---|---|---|---|---|---|---|
| | Japan | US | Japan | US | Japan | US |
| China | 0.14 | 0.12 | 0.22 | 0.12 | 0.18 | 0.10 |
| Korea | 0.25 | 0.23 | 0.24 | 0.23 | 0.20 | 0.18 |
| Hong Kong | 0.16 | 0.08 | 0.15 | 0.08 | 0.12 | 0.07 |
| Singapore | 0.20 | 0.16 | 0.21 | 0.15 | 0.17 | 0.15 |
| Thailand | 0.30 | 0.11 | 0.29 | 0.12 | 0.25 | 0.12 |
| Indonesia | 0.25 | 0.11 | 0.23 | 0.12 | 0.16 | 0.10 |
| Philippine | 0.18 | 0.20 | 0.22 | 0.18 | 0.19 | 0.17 |
| Malaysia | 0.24 | 0.17 | 0.27 | 0.16 | 0.21 | 0.17 |

*Source: Direction of Trade*, IMF

Between 1985 and 1997, the exports from East Asia marked a steady, five-fold increase (before declining in 1998 due to the Asian financial crisis), raising the share of exports in world total from 9 per cent in 1980–85 to 18 per cent in 1997 (see Kawai, 2004). At the same time, FDI inflows are expanding in East Asia hand-in-hand with trade. The share of FDI inflows to East Asia in world total increased from eight per cent in 1985 to 22 per cent in the mid-1990s, though it declined to 9 per cent in 2002.

The FDI to the Asian economies not only enlarged the exporting capacity, but also changed the trade structure of the region. As in the Fukao, et al. (2003) document, intra-industry trade increased for the past decades, following an increase in vertical FDI by US and Japanese multinational corporations. These multinational corporations relocated segments of their production rather than the entire industries, depending on the comparative advantage of each FDI recipient country (Hill and Athukorala, 1998). Hence, trade expansion in East Asia inevitably involved a rise in intra-industry trade. Athukorala (2003) has documented that expansion in fragmented trade is more evident in the East Asian region than in Europe or North America.

Japan's role as an FDI provider has also been increasing its importance in the region. Table 3 reports Japanese FDI (in terms of both its value and number of cases) in East Asia for the period between 1989 and 2002. The total value of Japanese direct investment flows to China, starting from a level slightly above the Philippines in 1989, hit its peak in 1995, exceeding far beyond twofold of those of other Asian countries. In terms of FDI cases, the growth of Japan's FDI to China is even more striking; in 1995, 27 per cent of Japanese total FDI is directed to China. Unquestionably, China has been the major recipient of Japanese FDI in the Asian region during the last decade.

Many researchers have investigated the trade-FDI nexus in the region, and claimed that the relationship has been bidirectional. That is, the Asian economies that implemented policies to create a friendly environment for FDI have been able to transform their industrial structures toward more export-oriented ones. Export expansion, in return, has had positive feedback effects and facilitated further liberalization of goods and financial trade. Financial liberalization has enabled countries to receive more FDI inflows. Petri (1995) presents empirical evidence in both the macro and the firm levels for this bidirectional relationship. Petri (1992) finds Japanese firms' FDI to Thailand enhanced trade between the two countries as well as trade between these two countries and the rest of the world, while Lee (1994) and Lin (1996) present evidence that the FDI from the home countries, Korea and Taiwan, respectively, promote only the bilateral trade volumes. Moreover, Kawai and Urata (1998) find a complementary relationship between Japan's exports and FDI to East Asia in food, textiles, chemical products, general machinery, and electronic machinery industries, while they also find that exports and FDI exhibit a strong negative relationship in wood and pulp industries. Dobson and Chia (1997), investigating intra-firm trade in East Asia, conclude that intra-firm trade tends to diminish as the host country's economy matures. They find that, as the host country develops and its domestic purchasing power rises, the direction of FDI shifts toward more sophisticated, or end-user type of products such as consumer durables. We must make one important point, however, that most of the empirical studies on the trade-FDI nexus are focusing on bilateral trade and FDI flows by heavily relying on the gravity model. Our study examines the dynamics of the trade-FDI nexus in a three country frame work.

## Triangular Trade Approach and Related Literature

When considering how to sell products in a foreign market, a multinational firm can choose whether to export the products directly from its home country, or produce them in the foreign market through its foreign subsidiaries. In the empirical trade literature, many researchers have attempted to answer the question of whether foreign production (i.e., FDI) and exports are substitutes or complements. Yamawaki (1991), Clausing (2000), and Head and Ries (2001) find that a complimentary relationship exists between foreign production and exports, whereas Belderbos and Sleuwaegen (1998) find that Japanese FDI and exports are substitutes only when the intention of FDI is to avoid antidumping tariffs in Europe. Blonigen (2001), using product-level data, finds FDI and exports are

(100 million Yen)

**Table 3.** Japanese foreign direct investment to the Asian countries (1989 – 2000)

| | 1989 | 1990 | 1991 | 1992 | 1993 | 1994 | 1995 | 1996 | 1997 | 1998 | 1999 | 2000 | 2001 | 2002 |
|---|---|---|---|---|---|---|---|---|---|---|---|---|---|---|
| China | 587 | 511 | 787 | 1,381 | 1,954 | 2,683 | 4,319 | 2,828 | 2,438 | 1,377 | 849 | 1,112 | 1,808 | 2,152 |
| | (126) | (165) | (246) | (490) | (700) | (636) | (770) | (365) | (258) | (114) | (78) | (105) | (189) | (263) |
| Korea | 799 | 419 | 357 | 291 | 289 | 420 | 433 | 468 | 543 | 389 | 1,094 | 899 | 704 | 763 |
| | (81) | (54) | (48) | (28) | (34) | (27) | (25) | (33) | (53) | (48) | (62) | (52) | (47) | (44) |
| H.K. | 2,502 | 2,610 | 1,260 | 966 | 1,447 | 1,179 | 1,106 | 1,675 | 860 | 789 | 1,088 | 1,039 | 374 | 248 |
| | (335) | (244) | (178) | (154) | (184) | (112) | (119) | (89) | (121) | (51) | (76) | (52) | (37) | (31) |
| Sing. | 2,573 | 1,232 | 837 | 875 | 735 | 1,101 | 1,143 | 1,256 | 2,238 | 832 | 1,102 | 505 | 1,433 | 915 |
| | (181) | (139) | (103) | (100) | (97) | (69) | (94) | (102) | (96) | (58) | (51) | (25) | (31) | (34) |
| Thai. | 1,703 | 1,696 | 1,107 | 849 | 680 | 749 | 1,196 | 1,581 | 2,291 | 1,760 | 924 | 1,030 | 1,105 | 614 |
| | (403) | (377) | (258) | (130) | (127) | (126) | (147) | (196) | (154) | (72) | (72) | (62) | (51) | (52) |
| Indon. | 840 | 1,615 | 1,628 | 2,142 | 952 | 1,808 | 1,548 | 2,720 | 3,085 | 1,398 | 1,024 | 464 | 622 | 509 |
| | (140) | (155) | (148) | (122) | (115) | (116) | (168) | (160) | (170) | (64) | (57) | (26) | (56) | (41) |
| Philip. | 269 | 383 | 277 | 210 | 236 | 683 | 692 | 630 | 642 | 488 | 689 | 514 | 951 | 500 |
| | (87) | (58) | (42) | (45) | (56) | (75) | (100) | (75) | (64) | (46) | (32) | (44) | (25) | (20) |
| Malay. | 902 | 1,067 | 1,202 | 919 | 892 | 772 | 555 | 644 | 971 | 668 | 588 | 256 | 320 | 98 |
| | (159) | (169) | (136) | (111) | (92) | (51) | (57) | (69) | (82) | (34) | (44) | (23) | (18) | (11) |
| World | 90,339 | 83,527 | 56,862 | 44,313 | 41,514 | 42,808 | 49,568 | 54,095 | 66,236 | 52,413 | 74,703 | 53,854 | 39,922 | 44,175 |
| | (6589) | (5863) | (4564) | (3741) | (3488) | (2478) | (2863) | (2501) | (2495) | (1616) | (1729) | (1701) | (1768) | (2144) |

*Source: Outward Direct Investment, Ministry of Finance, Japan. Figs. in parentheses indicate the number of FDI cases.*

substitutes when FDI is horizontal. However, these studies only focus on the relationship between outward FDI flows and exports.

Our framework is closer to Zhang and Felmingham (2001) who investigate the causal relationship between inward FDI to China and Chinese exports. Using data from both national and provincial levels, they confirm that the causal relationship is bidirectional. Especially for the causality from inward FDI flows to exports, they argue that foreign investors who have superior knowledge on world market conditions tend to export their products from the host country. In any case, these previous researches only looked at trade-FDI relationships between two countries.

In this paper we extend the investigation on the FDI-trade relationship to a three-country framework. Given the recent trends in international trade which involve a quite deal of intra-firm or intra-industry trade and FDI flows, we think that investigating the dynamics of trade in the conventional bilateral framework is not sufficient. In order to examine the dynamics of trade between China and the USA, we must incorporate the effects of third factors such as trade flows and FDI flows between China and other countries (than the USA). In what follows, we attempt to generalize the complex trilateral trade and FDI relationship, often called the 'export-platform FDI'.[1]

*Export-platform FDI: Vertical Foreign Direct Investment*

Let us consider the trade-FDI dynamics of one commodity among three countries: the USA, Japan, and a third country which we call China for now. For the sake of brevity, we assume that the USA provides a market for the commodity, and that Japan has a multinational firm that produces the commodity. The multinational firm may involve two firms for the production of the commodity: an upstream firm, U, and a downstream firm, D, while the former supplies intermediate goods to the latter and the latter sells the final product to the US market. If both downstream and upstream firms are established in Japan, the product will be exported directly from Japan to the USA. The trade dynamics of this first, base case are shown in Figure 1.a. Arrows in the figure represent the flows of goods. In this case international trade flows are purely bilateral between the USA and Japan, and involve no foreign production or FDI by the Japanese multinational.

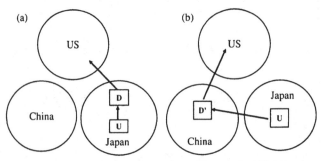

**Figure 1.** a. Trade flows prior to FDI. b. Trade flows after vertical FDI for down stream firm

Now, we consider a next case where the Japanese multinational makes vertical FDI.[2] The Japanese multinational firm fragments its production by establishing a downstream firm D in China as a vertical FDI, and exports the product from there. This case is depicted in Figure 1.b. We assume for simplicity that the domestic downstream plant D is shut down once the Japanese-affiliated plant D is established in China, and therefore that all of the exports come from D. This case leads to three changes in the trade flows among the three countries. First, Japanese exports to the USA stop because of the shut-down of the domestic plant D. Second, Japanese exports to China arise because of intra-firm trade between the parent firm U and its foreign affiliate D'. Third, Chinese exports to the USA emerge because the Japanese downstream plant in China starts shipping the product to the USA.

In reality, a trilateral relationship is not as clear-cut as is shown above. However, we can generally predict that if Japanese firms are shifting their production to China through vertical FDI, Japanese exports to the USA would decrease while both Japanese exports to China and Chinese exports to the USA increase. Thus, when vertical FDI is made, while Japanese exports of a certain product are observed to be decreasing, Japanese producers may be still exporting the same product to the USA, but by passing through China.

### Export-platform FDI: Non-fragmentation

The next case is one where the Japanese multinational makes export-platform FDI without fragmentation of production process. Figure 2.a depicts the base model for this case in which the Japanese multinational, M, exports its product directly to the USA. However, unlike the case in Figure 1.a, we assume that the multinational does not possess a vertical chain of production – the firm's production is vertically internalized. Figure 2.b shows the case where non-fragmentation occurs, so that the product is now being exported directly from China instead of Japan. In reality, as in Figure 1.b, the trade flows in this case would entail a decrease in Japanese direct exports to the USA and an increase in Chinese exports to the USA. However, unlike in the previous case, this case does not lead to any intra-firm trade between Japan and China.[3]

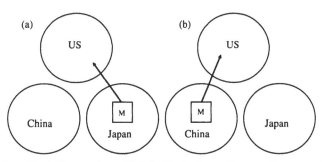

**Figure 2.** a. Trade flows prior to FDI. b. Trade flows after non-fragmentation FDI

*Do Imports Promote Export?*

Besides FDI flows, there are other factors that can affect the trilateral trade relationship. Some studies find that the imports of foreign products with higher quality can force domestic competitors to become more efficient through international competition. MacDonald (1994) finds that US industries' productivity level rose as the import penetration ratio increased (see also Galdon-Sanchez and Schmitz, 2002). Many studies also find that more efficient firms tend to export. Bernard and Jensen (1999) find that both the ex-ante growth rates and the levels of success measures are higher for exporters, i.e., 'good firms become exporters'. Combining these two findings and applying to our trilateral trade analysis, we can hypothesize that an increase in the exports from a Japanese firm (JPN) to China may lead a Chinese domestic firm (CHN) to become more efficient and start exporting. This case is shown in Figure 3. Although the trade flows look similar to the case in Figure 1.b, this case does not involve any FDI flows.

*Competition or Complements*

Last, but not least, we can think of a case where Japanese exports to the USA and Chinese exports to the USA are substitutes. This is highly probable for an industry in which the exports of the two countries are similar in quality (see Figure 4). In this case, head-to-head competition may arise between Japanese and Chinese firms, which can be observed as a negative correlation between Japanese and Chinese exports to the USA.

   We must also consider that Japanese and Chinese exports to the USA could have a complementary relationship if both countries produce intermediate products, and export them to the US market where a firm in the USA assembles the final goods using the intermediate products. In this case, we should observe a positive correlation between Japanese and Chinese exports to the USA. It is, however, unlikely to find products from two countries to be compatable if we use data based on the industry classification as aggregated as the HS 4-digit level, which we use in our study. Therefore, we should expect to find a negative correlation between Japanese and Chinese exports to the USA with an assumption that the competitive effect outweighs the complimentary effect.

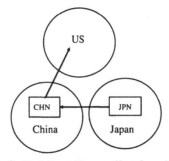

**Figure 3.** Positive spillover effect from imports

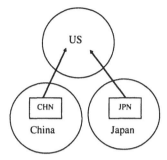

**Figure 4.** Competition (substitutive relationship): negative correlation

## The 'Triangular Trade Approach'

The above discussions have shown the complexity of the trade-FDI dynamics, but also demonstrated that we can unravel the complex dynamics by examining the relationships between different flows of trade among the three countries. Figure 5 presents a generic export flow chart among the three countries. The Japanese exports to the USA and those to China are denoted as JPNUS and JPNCHN, respectively, while the Chinese exports to the USA is denoted as CHNUS.

Table 4 summarizes all the scenarios we discussed and expected signs for the correlations between two of the three trade flows. As for the relationship between JPNCHN and CHNUS, we should expect a positive correlation if vertical FDI is made by Japanese firms to China or if Japanese exports to China create spillover effects on Chinese firms and lead them to export to the USA. As for the relationship between JPNUS and CHNUS, we should expect a negative correlation if vertical or non-fragmentation FDI is made by Japanese firms to China or if the products from China and Japan are in direct competition in the US market.

In this study, we will employ what we call the 'triangular trade approach,' in which we will examine the type of trade-FDI dynamics by empirically looking at the correlations between the trade flows in the trilateral trade relationship between Japan, the USA, and China (or other Asian 'third countries'). More

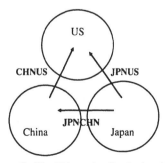

**Figure 5.** The Triangular Trade Approach

**Table 4.** Expected signs for the correlation between trade flows

| | Expected signs for the correlation between | |
| --- | --- | --- |
| | JPNCHN and CHNUS | JPNUS and CHNUS |
| Vertical FDI | Positive | Negative |
| Non-fragmentation FDI | — | Negative |
| Imports-Exports | Positive | — |
| Competition | — | Positive |

*Note*: The cells with '−' indicate that there is no specific theoretical prediction for the sign of the correlation.

specifically, we will use the export flow from China, or third countries, to the USA (CHNUS or THDUS) as the dependent variable in the empirical model while including Japan's exports to China, or the third countries (JPNCHN or JPNTHD) as well as Japan's exports to the USA (JPNUS) as explanatory variables. By comparing what we find in the empirical analysis with the theoretical predictions in Table 4, we will conjecture what kind of trade and/or FDI relationship exists between the countries.

## Data

The exports data used in this study are extracted at the HS 4-digit level from *International Trade by Commodity Statistics (ITCS), Harmonized System Rev.1*, OECD. At this level of disaggregation, there are 1,367 commodity classifications. From this set of data, we select our sample in the following two steps. First, we remove the commodities which have missing values in *any* of the years in our sample period of 1990 through 2000. We also restrict our sample to comprise the commodities for which a complete set of observations exists with a strictly positive amount of trade for the entire sample period. Second, we need three flows of exports for each of the third countries, that is, Japanese exports to the third country; Japanese exports to the USA; and the third country's exports to the USA. As such, we restrict our data to only those commodities for which *all of the three* export flows exist. This selection process causes the number of observations to decline considerably and to vary among the third countries depending on data availability. The number of commodities for the third countries are 576 for China, 572 for Korea, 487 for Hong Kong, 288 for Singapore, 310 for Thailand, 162 for Indonesia, 180 for the Philippines, and 218 for Malaysia.

Annual observations of exchange rate volatility are constructed from monthly exchange rates from IMF's *International Financial Statistics*. Other macroeconomic variables are retrieved from IMF's *IFS* and *Direction of Trade*. We also include the trade intensity indices for each pair of trading countries using the method in Frankel and Rose (1997). More details on the data definitions are given in the Appendix.

## Empirical Results With the Base Model

### Model Specification and Empirical Results

First, we specify a general error component regression model for the panel dataset using the first-differenced trilateral trade flows as shown in Equation (1).

$$\Delta T_{i,j,t}^{THDUS} = \sum_{i=1}^{I} \alpha_i D^i \Delta T_{i,j,t}^{JPNTHD} + \sum_{i=1}^{I} \beta_i D^i \Delta T_{i,j,t}^{JPNUS} + \sum_{k=1}^{K} \phi_k Z_{i,t}^k$$

$$+ \lambda_{i,j} + \varepsilon_{i,j,t}.\, i = 1, \ldots, I;\, j(i) = 1, \ldots, J(i);\, t = 1, \ldots, T \tag{1}$$

$\Delta T_{i,j,t}^{THDUS}$ is the first-differenced exports of third country $i$ to the USA for commodity $j$ at year $t$, while $\Delta T_{i,j,t}^{JPNTHD}$ and $\Delta T_{i,j,t}^{JPNUS}$ are the first-differenced Japanese exports to the third country and those to the USA, respectively. The dummy variable $D^i$ takes a value of unity for country $i$ and zero otherwise, and is also included to allow for heterogeneous coefficients for the export variables. $Z_{i,t}^k$ represents a $k$-th exogenous variable for country $i$ at year $t$. $\lambda_{i,j}$ is the individual effect while $\varepsilon_{i,j,t}$ is the disturbance term. We should note that the number of commodities, $J(i)$, varies for each third country $i$, and that we suppress $(i)$ for the subscript $j$ in the notation.

To select our model specification between random effect and fixed effect models, we use Arellano's (1993) Wald test because it is robust to heteroskedasticity and autocorrelation of the disturbances.[4] If the null hypothesis that the conditional expectation of the unobserved individual effects is zero is rejected, we will use the fixed effect model. Otherwise, we will use the random effect model. If the LM heteroskedasticity test statistics or Bhargava-DW statistics from the within estimation indicate that the disturbances entail heteroskedasticity or serial autocorrelation, we will use the White heterosckedasticity-consistent standard deviations.

### Preliminary Analysis With Only Export Variables

First, as a preliminary analysis, we include only the export variables in our panel data estimation as shown in Equation (2). Because the robust Arellano statistic is found to reject the null hypothesis significantly, we use the fixed effect model. Also, since the LM test statistics indicate that the model specification entails heteroskedasticity and serial correlation, we use the White standard deviations.

$$\Delta T_{i,j,t}^{THDUS} = \sum_{i=1}^{8} \alpha_i D^i \Delta T_{i,j,t}^{JPNTHD} + \sum_{i=1}^{8} \beta_i D^i \Delta T_{i,j,t}^{JPNUS} + \lambda_{i,j} + \varepsilon_{i,j,t} \tag{2}$$

$$i = 1, \ldots, 8;\, j(i) = 1, \ldots, J(i);\quad t = 1, \ldots, 10$$

Table 5 reports the estimation results. The estimated coefficients of Japanese exports to third countries (JPNTHD) are always positive. While the magnitude of the coefficients varies among the third countries, it is especially higher for Korea (0.30), Singapore (0.32), and Malaysia (0.73), more than tenfold of the coefficients for Hong Kong, Thailand, and Indonesia. However, we obtained statistically significant coefficients only for China, Korea, and Malaysia.

This preliminary analysis shows that Japan's exports to some of the Asian countries are positively correlated with their exports to the USA. Previously, we discussed a possibility of technology transfer from an exporting country to an importing country. However, we should not exclude a possibility of FDI affecting the correlations either.

Our previous discussion suggests that the expected sign for the coefficient of JPNUS (Japanese exports to the USA) can be negative in the following two cases. First, it can be negative when the two countries' exports are competing head-to-head in US markets. Second, when Japanese companies are shifting their production bases from Japan to their subsidiaries in the third country, which inevitably involves FDI by the parent firms, their direct exports from Japan to the USA can be replaced with those from the third country. However, we must also note that the sign can be positive when some common factors, such as high US economic growth, are causing both flows of exports to increase.

Interestingly, the estimated coefficient of JPNUS is significantly negative only for China (−0.05). We can surmise that this is either because Japanese and Chinese exporters competing head-to-head or because Japanese multinational

**Table 5.** Within estimates from the triangular trade regression [Dependent variable: (first-differenced) exports of third countries to the USA]

| Variable | Coefficient | Variable | Coefficient |
|---|---|---|---|
| JPNCHN | 0.125** | JPNUS(CHN) | −0.048* |
| | (0.063) | | (0.028) |
| JPNKOR | 0.301** | JPNUS(KOR) | 0.215*** |
| | (0.122) | | (0.069) |
| JPNHKG | 0.071 | JPNUS(HKG) | 0.022 |
| | (0.068) | | (0.016) |
| JPNSGP | 0.319 | JPNUS(SGP) | 0.082 |
| | (0.246) | | (0.098) |
| JPNTHA | 0.006 | JPNUS(THA) | 0.024 |
| | (0.035) | | (0.015) |
| JPNIDN | 0.024 | JPNUS(IDN) | −0.004 |
| | (0.017) | | (0.006) |
| JPNPHL | 0.161 | JPNUS(PHL) | −0.024 |
| | (0.369) | | (0.023) |
| JPNMAL | 0.732*** | JPNUS(MAL) | 0.053 |
| | (0.245) | | (0.040) |
| NOB = 27930 | Adj. $R^2$ = 0.350 | | |

*Note*: All trade-related variables are included as first-differenced variables. White heteroskedasticity consistent standard deviations are in parentheses. ***, **, and * denote significance at 1, 5, and 10 per cent levels, respectively. The number of commodities differs for each country due to the data selection process which is explained in the 'Data' section. The number of commodities is 576 for China, 572 for Korea, 487 for Hong Kong, 288 for Singapore, 310 for Thailand, 162 for Indonesia, 180 for the Philippines, and 218 for Malaysia.

corporations are shifting their production bases from Japan to China through FDI. However, we cannot yet tell which hypothesis is applicable.

*Analysis With Country Characteristics As Explanatory Variables*

In this section, following the gravity model literature, we include macroeconomic variables in addition to JPNTHD and JPNUS (see Appendix). After dropping some of the variables that appeared to cause multicollinearity, we decided to include 10 macro variables in $Z_{i,t}$ (equation (1)).[5]

Past empirical studies on bilateral trade relationships suggest the effects of macro control variables as follows. The inflation rate in a third country is expected to be negatively correlated to the country's exports to the US because of an increase in the overall costs in the third country. While US nominal GDP should be positively correlated with third countries' exports to the USA, the effect of Japan's nominal GDP on third countries' exports to the USA depends on whether the exports from Japan and the third countries are complements or substitutes. The effect can be positive (but indirectly) if the exports from the third country and Japan are complements, but negative if they are substitutes. Other Japan-related macroeconomic variables are difficult to make a priori assumptions here.

Table 6 shows the estimation results from the analysis with macroeconomic variables. Unlike past findings in the literature, most of the macroeconomic variables are insignificant. Moreover, the estimated coefficients for JPNTHD and JPNUS are unaffected while the adjusted R-squared barely improve. We suspect that the reason why these macroeconomic variables do not improve the estimation is because some of the variables take only a small number of different values while trade-related data vary depending on the third country ($i$) and the commodity ($j$). For example, there are only 10 different (i.e., annual) values for USA nominal GDP in a sample of 27,930 observations. We should note the explanatory power of macroeconomic variables in the past bilateral trade studies hinges on the use of aggregated trade data. As such, we need to employ some other data that entail more variation.

## Empirical Results With More Disaggregated Variables

Given the above discussion, we re-estimate our model using more disaggregated data as control variables. Instead of the macroeconomic variables, we include US total imports on commodity basis (i.e., disaggregated at the HS 4-digit level) to control for changes in US demand for each commodity, and Japanese FDI (at the HS 2-digit level) to capture some possible production shift by Japanese multinational corporations.

*Data Construction*

For the variable on US disaggregated imports, we use the same dataset from OECD's *ITCS* and call it USMAR. We hope that this variable will be a good proxy

**Table 6.** Within estimates for the triangular trade regression with macro variables [Dependent variable: (first-differenced) exports of third countries to the USA]

| Variable | Coefficient | Variable | Coefficient | Variable | Coefficient |
|---|---|---|---|---|---|
| JPNCHN | 0.109* | JPNUS(CHN) | − 0.049* | EXVOL_US | − 6,347 |
| | (0.063) | | (0.028) | | (9,781) |
| JPNKOR | 0.299** | JPNUS(KOR) | 0.215*** | INF_THD | − 0.631 |
| | (0.124) | | (0.069) | | (52) |
| JPNHKG | 0.074 | JPNUS(HKG) | 0.023 | INF_US | 457 |
| | (0.069) | | (0.016) | | (1,118) |
| JPNSGP | 0.319 | JPNUS(SGP) | 0.082 | NY_THD | − 0.016 |
| | (0.246) | | (0.098) | | (0.012) |
| JPNTHA | 0.018 | JPNUS(THA) | 0.024 | NY_US | 0.007 |
| | (0.036) | | (0.015) | | (0.005) |
| JPNIDN | 0.031* | JPNUS(IDN) | − 0.003 | NY_JPN | − 0.002 |
| | (0.018) | | (0.006) | | (0.002) |
| JPNPHL | 0.171 | JPNUS(PHL) | − 0.022 | W_IMP_THD | 0.069** |
| | (0.367) | | (0.022) | | (0.032) |
| JPNMAL | 0.733*** | JPNUS(MAL) | 0.052 | W_IMP_JPN | − 0.055 |
| | (0.245) | | (0.040) | | (0.044) |
| | | | | W_EXP_THD | 0.251*** |
| | | | | | (0.061) |
| | | | | W_EXP_US | − 0.011 |
| | | | (0.030) | | |
| NOB = 27930 | | Adj. R2 = 0.351 | | | |

*Note*: See notes below Table 5.

for actual expenditure allocated for each imported commodity. Unlike the macroeconomic variables, this variable takes as many different values as the dependent variable.

Given our suspicion in the previous analysis that the estimated coefficient of JPNTHD may have reflected the effect of Japanese FDI flows to the third countries, we include a variable that specifically refers to Japanese FDI to the third countries. For this variable, we use the data from the *Overseas Japanese Companies Data (OJCD)* from Toyo Keizai. OJCD contains the information for approximately 19,000 Japanese overseas subsidiaries, categorized in 68 industry classifications (which do not correspond to HS industry classifications), including each subsidiary's established year, location, business objectives, industry classification, and other relevant information. Among the 68 industries, we exclude those industries which do not actively engage in goods trade such as real estate and banking sectors. Then, we reallocate OJCD's codes to corresponding HS 2-digit codes and reclassify the data to create the FDI data based on the HS classifications. The new variable counts as Japanese FDI in the Asian third countries, the number of the subsidiaries established by Japanese firms for each host country, year, and HS 2-digit industry code.[6]

*Estimation Results*

With these two additional variables, our estimation model becomes:

$$\Delta T_{i,j,t}^{THDUS} = \sum_{i=1}^{8} \alpha_i D^i \Delta T_{i,j,t}^{JPNTHD} + \sum_{i=1}^{8} \beta_i D^i \Delta T_{i,j,t}^{JPNUS} \sum_{i=1}^{8} \delta_i D^i FDI_{i,j,t}$$

$$+ \sum_{i=1}^{8} \gamma_i D^i \Delta USMAR_{i,j,t} + \lambda_{i,j} + \varepsilon_{i,j,t}$$

$$i = 1, \ldots, 8; j(i) = 1, \ldots, J(i); \quad t = 1, \ldots, 10$$

(3)

The estimation results are shown in Table 7. As for the US disaggregated import variables, USMAR, many of the coefficients are significantly positive. Among the Japanese FDI variables, the coefficient is significantly positive only for China, indicating that Japanese multinationals' FDI to China complements Chinese exports to the USA. Interestingly, with this model specification, the estimated coefficient for the Japanese exports to China is no longer significant, a stark contrast with the previous analysis where Japanese exports to China appeared to be promoting Chinese exports to the USA. Given this and the previous results, we can surmise that Chinese exports to the USA grow only through relocation of Japanese production plants to China (implemented through FDI), not from indirect technology transfer through Japanese exports.

The triangular trade relationships involving Korea and Indonesia cast an interesting contrast to the case with China. The coefficients of the Japanese exports variables to these two countries remain significant at the five per cent significance level while the coefficients of the FDI variables are not significant. This means that for Korea and Indonesia, Japanese exports to these countries are positively correlated with their exports to the USA while Japanese FDI does not seem to play any important role in promoting these countries' exports to the USA. The positive coefficients for the Japanese exports to Korea and Indonesia can be attributed to technology transfer or competitive pressure from Japanese exports to these countries.

In contrast to the previous results shown in Table 5, the coefficients of JPNUS are also significantly negative for not only China but also Indonesia and the Philippines. Moreover, the Korean coefficient for JPNUS, which was significantly positive in the previous estimation, is no longer significant. We believe that including the USMAR variable eliminates the positive income effect of US market growth from JPNUS. It is noteworthy that the absolute value of JPNUS's coefficient for China is much larger than that of Indonesia or the Philippines. Therefore, we can conclude that the degree of competition with Japanese products in US markets is much higher for Chinese exports than the other countries'.[7]

**Table 7.** Within estimates from the triangular trade regression with FDI and USA market size [Dependent variable: (first-differenced) exports of third countries to the USA]

| Variable | Coefficient | Variable | Coefficient | Variable | Coefficient | Variable | Coefficient |
|---|---|---|---|---|---|---|---|
| JPNCHN | 0.038 (0.067) | JPNUS(CHN) | −0.141*** (0.044) | FDICHN | 51.358*** (15) | USMAR(CHN) | 0.052*** (0.016) |
| JPNKOR | 0.202** (0.095) | JPNUS(KOR) | 0.055 (0.050) | FDIKOR | −531.120 (522) | USMAR(KOR) | 0.093*** (0.024) |
| JPNHKG | 0.048 (0.069) | JPNUS(HKG) | 0.012 (0.012) | FDIHKG | −42.172 (54) | USMAR(HKG) | 0.006 (0.004) |
| JPNSGP | 0.263 (0.224) | JPNUS(SGP) | 0.063 (0.110) | FDISGP | −107.803 (231) | USMAR(SGP) | 0.017 (0.016) |
| JPNTHA | −0.002 (0.031) | JPNUS(THA) | 0.013 (0.019) | FDITHA | −27.908 (23) | USMAR(THA) | 0.006 (0.005) |
| JPNIDN | 0.026** (0.011) | JPNUS(IDN) | −0.020*** (0.008) | FDIIDN | −76.020 (72) | USMAR(IDN) | 0.008*** (0.003) |
| JPNPHL | −0.003 (0.345) | JPNUS(PHL) | −0.083*** (0.032) | FDIPHL | 90.768 (175) | USMAR(PHL) | 0.031** (0.013) |
| JPNMAL | 0.440** (0.224) | JPNUS(MAL) | −0.041 (0.042) | FDIMAL | −647.534*** (212) | USMAR(MAL) | 0.068*** (0.022) |

NOB = 27930    Adj.R2 = 0.445

*Note:* See notes below Table 5.

**Discussions**

In this paper, we examined the effect of export-platform FDI on international trade. On issues related to FDI determination, there has been much theoretical work done. Helpman (1984) developed a model to explain the dynamics of vertical FDI while Markusen (1984) focused on horizontal FDI. Only recently, did Motta and Norman (1996) provide theoretical foundations for export-platform FDI, followed by many others who have presented equilibrium outcomes of FDI decision makings with respect to different parameter values for transport cost, tariffs, and set-up costs. While the literature on FDI issues tends to focus on the determinants of FDI, the contribution of our paper is that we examine FDI as a variable that affects the structure of international trade. We believe that the link between export-platform FDI and international trade in our context will stimulate further theoretical development in the literature.

In our empirical investigation, we found that the exports of China and those of Japan are directly competing in US markets while the former seems to be partly promoted by Japanese exports to China. However, after controlling for Japan's FDI to China, the trade-enhancing effect of Japanese exports disappears, but instead, Japanese FDI to China enters statistically significantly. This result allows us to conclude that Japanese exports to China promote Chinese exports to the USA through increased vertical trade between Japanese multinationals and their affiliates in China. The evidence of the substitutive relationship between Chinese and Japanese exports in US markets along with the export-promoting effect of Japanese FDI to China confirms a view that Japanese multinationals are shifting their production bases to China as a means to diversify their global production network.

In our estimation results for other Asian countries, we show that Indonesian and Philippine exports are also competing with Japanese exports in US markets. However, the degree of the competition with Japanese exports is found to be much higher for China. Also, the coefficients for Japanese FDI to these countries are found to be positive, but insignificant, indicating that Japanese FDI to these countries is not promoting the countries' exports to the USA. Thus, the export-platform FDI argument with relevance to the US market is only applicable to China, but not to other Asian countries. This finding is consistent with Markusen and Maskus (2002).

We think the methodology we employed in this paper is applicable to other economic regions. One good candidate area would be Latin America. In this region, we can replace Japan with the USA as the main FDI provider in the region. We can casually suspect that this type of examination on the Latin American region may reveal some evidence for export-platform FDI as we have observed in the Asian region. The approach could also be applied to the East European region where Germany can be the regional FDI provider.

*Political Implications*

In the last two decades, international trade with China has expanded rapidly while the Chinese economy experienced unprecedented high growth. Between 1992 and

2000, Chinese exports almost tripled from \$84.9 billion to \$249 billion, as did Chinese imports (from \$80.6 billion to \$225 billion). With the accession to the WTO in 2001, China's trade is expected to experience an even higher growth in the years to come.

China's significant presence in the world trade has also given a rise to new trade disputes with trading partners, especially the United States. China is not only condemned for threatening trading partners' industries with its mighty exports, but also for its currency policy which allegedly maintains Chinese renminbi at an artificially low value to help its exports. The recent protectionist debate in the US Congress about whether to impose restrictions on textile imports from China, unless the latter alters its exchange rate policy, exemplifies political concerns over a loss of manufacturing jobs in US industries due to rising manufacturing imports from China.[8]

To many, these trade issues between the USA and China are reminiscent of the trade conflicts between the USA and Japan that lasted until recently. For decades, both academic and policy making circles intensely debated on foreign access to Japanese markets as well as Japanese exporters' allegedly 'unfair' trade practices in textile, automobile, and semiconductors, among many others, that were claimed to have hurt US industries. There is, however, only one trade dispute case against Japan, brought by the USA, to the WTO dispute settlement mechanism between 1999 and 2003. The intensity of the bilateral trade disputes waned in the last decade, partly due to the decade-long recession in Japan, and more importantly, to the emergence of China as the world exporter.

Trade conflicts between countries could change their forms and players as the tide in foreign direct investment changes its direction. For example, a decrease in the exports of a country might merely be a reflection of global production shift by the country's multinational corporations. Although we witness the 'threat' of Japanese exports diminishing, and the threat of Chinese exports rising, some portion of Chinese exports to the USA may include products made by Japanese affiliates in China (which appear with the label 'made in China' instead of 'made in Japan'). In fact, Japan's Ministry of Finance reported that the number of new outflow foreign direct investment (FDI) cases by Japanese firms to China exceeded those to the USA in 1994, 1995 and 2002.

## *Implications for Management, Business and Readers*

Our findings confirmed the anecdote that multinationals are racing to set up production facilities in China to make the best and most use of inexpensive Chinese labour. The flip side of it is that part of the Chinese exporting capacities is dependent on multinational corporations. As of now, it is safe to conjecture that Chinese exporting industries are growing by absorbing production technology and managerial skills from multinational corporations. This also means that the continuing dissemination or localization of technology and skills will help Chinese industry grow further and the quality of Chinese workers further improve. In other words, multinational corporations from the west and Japan can contribute to creating competitive Chinese firms. In 2003, for example, automobile production in China became the fourth largest just following after the USA, Japan and Germany. Within a decade it is most likely to see Chinese brand automobiles flooding to developed countries.

History has already shown examples of countries that took off from the developmental stage by initially taking the advantage of inexpensive labour and later absorbing developed technology from the developed world. Recent examples before China include its current FDI-provider, Japan. However, the biggest difference between these two countries is that reliance on importation of advanced technology and managerial skills is greater in the case of China than that of Japan. However, the greater reliance on importation of knowledge and technology can be tricky. On the one hand, it can contribute to faster development of industries and firms. However, on the other hand, fast penetration of technology and knowledge may lead to faster improvement in productivity, thereby faster increases in the wages of skilled workers which may even lead to a loss of the country's initial attractiveness. *The Economist (2005)* argues that some multinational corporations already left China for Cambodia and Vietnam to look for cheaper labour forces. Considering that China provides a large amount of FDI to Southeast Asian countries, it may not take a long time for China to become another Japan.

**Conclusions**

While US current account deficits have expanded for the last few years, China has expanded its current account surpluses against the USA. Many observers claim that China manipulates the value of Renminbi to keep it at an unfairly low level against US dollars. While this argument can be a matter of macroeconomic misalignment, the issue of current account imbalance between the USA and China is far from extricable.

Our study shed light on the trade disputes between the two countries from a different angle and presented results that may involve important political ramifications. That is, based on our empirical results, a surge in Chinese exports to the USA may involve a large volume of products manufactured by Japanese affiliates in China and therefore may simply reflect some change in Japanese multinationals' global production strategy, not so much of the advent of the 'threat' of Chinese industrialization. With the American general perception of China 'threatening' US industry, there continue to be cases against China brought by the USA into the WTO, but more likely involving products of Japanese multinational corporations, at least for some foreseeable future.

It is becoming more likely that China revalues its currency or let it completely float eventually[9]. However, even after some change in Chinese exchange rate policy, foreign multinationals will probably continue exporting their products from China to the USA. It seems to be only some weakening of foreign multinationals' incentives to produce in China that may mitigate the current trend of US–China trade imbalances. However, it is also worthwhile to note that any decline in Chinese exports to the USA is likely to be matched by some increase in the exports from other parts of the world. Again, it seems to be multinational corporations that really matter.

## Acknowledgements

The earlier version of this paper was circulated under the title 'How Does China Compete with Japan in the US Market?: A Triangular Approach.' This research was conducted in part while Yushi Yoshida was a visiting research associate at the University of California, Santa Cruz. We would like to thank participants of the APEC Study Center Conference at City University of Hong Kong, the Japan Economic Association Conference at Meiji Gakuin University, the 'WTO, China and the Asian Economies II' Conference at Renmin University of China, and the 6th ETSG Conference at the University of Nottingham. We would also like to thank Eiji Fujii, Kui Wai Li, and anonymous referees for their insightful comments.

## Notes

[1] The seminal theoretical work in this literature is Motta and Norman (1996) who investigate various patterns of investment strategies by multinational firms by applying game theory in a three-country framework. Other important works include Neary (2002), Yeaple (2003), Ekholm *et al.*, (2003) and Grossman *et al.*, (2003). The studies, however, focus on describing equilibrium regimes for different set of parameter ranges, but fail to discuss the dynamics of trade and FDI flows in our context.

[2] We can also consider the case in which the multinational firm shifts its upstream firm to the local market. However, this case does not alter the nature of the existing trade flows.

[3] The presence of foreign affiliates can also create spillover effects on local exporters. Javorcik (2004) finds evidence for positive spillover effects of foreign affiliates on their local suppliers. Spillovers from foreign affiliates can help local firms not only to improve their productivity level, but also to become competitive exporters in the international markets. In such a case, we can expect an increase in the exports of the FDI-receiving country.

[4] While many researcher use the Hausman (1978) method which employs both GLS and within estimators for the specification test on random effects, Hausman and Taylor (1981) show that alternative test statistics incorporating the between estimators are also numerically identical. However, these tests are no longer valid if the disturbances are heteroskedastic and/or serially correlated, which we suspect in our data. For the summary of Hausman's specification test, see Baltagi (2001). Also, see Ahn and Low (1996) and Baltagi *et al.*, (2003) for recent developments of the specification tests.

[5] These variables are exchange rate volatility (EXVOL_US), inflation rate of the third countries (INF_THD), US inflation rate (INF_US), nominal GDP of the third countries (NY_THD), US nominal GDP (NY_US), Japanese nominal GDP (NY_JPN), third countries' imports from the world (W_IMP_THD), Japanese imports from the world (W_IMP_JPN), third countries' exports to the world (W_EXP_THD), and US exports to the world (W_EXP_US).

[6] The concordance table is available from authors upon request. When a particular OJCD code covers more than two HS 2-digit codes, the FDI data for this OJCD code is counted in all corresponding HS 2-digit codes. Therefore, two different HS 4-digit codes with the same first two digits share the same number of accumulated Japanese affiliated firms. This may not be problematic as long as there is cross-industry effect within the HS 2-digit level since we are trying to capture the trade-promoting effect of FDI.

[7] We also investigated equation (3) with the macroeconomic variables and found the results qualitatively unchanged. However, the Chinese coefficient for the FDI variable becomes statistically insignificant, though its *p*-value is about 14.8%. The estimation results are available upon request.

[8] See *The Economist's* articles, 'What do yuant from us?,' May 18, 2005 and 'Putting up the barricades,' April 21, 2005 as well as the US Congressional Budget Office's testimony on April 14, 2005. A list of other manufacturing products under debates between the two countries includes bedroom furniture, television sets, handbags, and handcarts among many others.

[9] While making final revisions to this paper, on July 21, 2005, China revalued Renminbi by 2.1 per cent against US dollars and moved to managed floating with a currency board system based on an unspecified basket of currencies that allows the currency to fluctuate within 0.3-per cent bands.

## References

Ahn, Seung C. & Low, S. (1996) A reformulation of the Hausman test for regression models with pooled cross-section-time-series data, *Journal of Econometrics*, 71, pp. 309–319.

Arellano, Manuel (1993) On the testing of correlated effects with panel data, *Journal of Econometrics*, 59, pp. 87–97.

Athukorala, Prema-chandra (2003) Product Fragmentation and Trade Patterns in East Asia, Australia National University, Working Paper 2003/21.

Baltagi, B. H. (2001) *Econometric Analysis of Panel Data* (Wiley: Chichester).

Baltagi, B. H., Bresson, G. & Pirotte, A. (2003) Fixed effects, random effects or Hausman-Taylor? A pretest estimator, *Economics Letters*, 79, pp. 361–369.

Bernard, A. B. & Bradford Jensen, J. (1999) Exceptional exporter performance: Cause, effect, or both?, *Journal of International Economics*, 47, pp. 1–25.

Belderbos, R. & Sleuwaegen, L. (1998) Tariff jumping DFI and export substitution: Japanese electronics firms in Europe, *International Journal of Industrial Organization*, 16, pp. 601–638.

Blonigen, B. A. (2001) In search of substitution between foreign production and exports, *Journal of International Economics*, 53, pp. 81–104.

Clausing, K. A. (2000) Does multinational activity displace trade?, *Economic Inquiry*, 38(2), pp. 190–205.

Congressional Budget Office (2005) Economic Relationships between the United States and China – Before the Committee on Ways and Means, US House of Representatives, April 14.

Dobson, W. & Chia, Siow Yue (1997) *Multinationals and East Asian integration* (Singapore: Institute of Southeast Asian Studies).

*Economist* (2005) China's People Problem, April 14th.

Ekholm, K., Forslid, R. & Markusen, J. R. (2003) Export-platform foreign direct investment, *NBER Working Paper* No.9517.

Frankel, J. & Andrew K., Rose (1997) The endogeneity of the optimum currency area criteria, mimeo.

Fukao, Kyoji, Hikari, Ishido & Keiko, Ito (2003) Vertical Intra-industry Trade and Foreign Direct Investment in East Asia, *Journal of the Japanese and International Economies*, 17(4), pp. 468–506.

Fung, K. C. & Iizaka, Hitomi (1998) Japanese and US trade with China: A comparative Analysis, *Review of Development Economics*, 2(2), pp. 181–190.

Galdon-Sanchez, J. E. & Schmitz, Jr, J. A. (2002) Competitive pressure and labour productivity: World iron-ore markets in the 1980's, *American Economic Review*, 92(4), pp. 1222–1235.

Grossman, G., Helpman, E. & Szeidl, A. (2003) Optimal integration strategies of US multinational Firm, NBER Working Paper No.10189.

Hausman, J. A. (1978) Specification tests in econometrics, *Econometrica*, 46, pp. 1251–1271.

Hausman, J. A. & Taylor, W. E. (1981) Panel data and unobservable individual effects, *Econometrica*, 49, pp. 1377–1398.

Head, K. & Ries, J. (2001) Overseas investment and firm exports, *Review of International Economics*, 9, pp. 108–122.

Helpman, Elhanan (1984) A simple theory of international trade with multinational corporations, *Journal of Political Economy*, 92, pp. 451–471.

Hill, Hal & Prema-chandra Athukorala (1998) Foreign Investment in East Asia: A Survey, *Asia-Pacific Literature*, 12(2), pp. 23–50.

Javorcik, Beata S. (2004) Does foreign direct investment increase the productivity of domestic firms? In search of spillovers through backward linkages, *American Economic Review*, 94(3), pp. 605–627.

Kawai, Masahiro (2004) Trade and Investment Integration for Development in East Asia: A Case for the Trade-FDI Nexus (Mimeo: University of Tokyo).

Kawai, M. & Urata, Shujiro (1998) Are Trade and Direct Foreign Investment Substitutes or Complements? An Empirical Analysis of Japanese Manufacturing Industries, in: Hiro Lee & D. W. Roland-Holst (Eds) *Economic Development and Cooperation in the Pacific Basin: Trade Investment, and Environmental Issues*, pp. 251–293 (Cambridge, UK: Cambridge University Press).

Lee, C. H. (1994) Korea's Direct Foreign Investment in Southeast Asia, *ASEAN Economic Bulletin*, 10(3), pp. 286–296.

Lin, A. L. (1996) Trade Effects of Foreign Direct Investment: Evidence for Taiwan with Four ASEAN Countries, *Weltwirtschaftliches Archiv*, 132(4), pp. 737–747.

MacDonald, J. M. (1994) Does import competition force efficient production?, *The Review of Economics and Statistics*, 76(4), pp. 721–727.

Markusen, J. R. (1984) Multinationals, multi-plant economies, and the gains from trade, *Journal of International Economics*, 31, pp. 205–226.

Markusen, J. R. & Maskus, K. E. (2002) Discriminating among alternative theories of the multinational enterprise, *Review of International Economics*, 10(4), pp. 694–707.

Motta, M. & Norman, G. (1996) Does economic integration cause foreign direct investment?, *International Economic Review*, 37(4), pp. 757–783.

Neary, J. P. (2002) Foreign direct investment and the single market, *The Manchester School*, 70(3), pp. 291–314.

Petri, P. A. (1992) Platforms in the Pacific: the Trade Effects of Direct Investment in Thailand, *Journal of Asian Economics.*, 3(2), pp. 173–196.

Petri, P. A. (1995) The interdependencies of trade and investment in the Pacific, in: E. K. Y. Chen & P. Drysdale (Eds) *Corporate and foreign direct investment in Asia and the Pacific*.

Yamawaki, Hideki (1991) Exports and foreign distributional activities: Evidence on Japanese firms in the United States, *The Review of Economics and Statistics*, 73(2), pp. 294–300.

Yeaple, S. R. (2003) The complex integration strategies of multinationals and cross country dependencies in the structure of foreign direct investment, *Journal of International Economics*, 60, pp. 293–314.

Zhang, Qing & Felmingham, B. (2001) The relationship between inward direct foreign investment and China's provincial export trade, *China Economic Review*, 12, pp. 82–89.

# Appendix:

exvol_US = exchange volatility between THD's currency and the US dollars
exvol_JPN = exchange volatility between THD's currency and Japanese yen
inf_THD = THD's inflation rate
inf_US = US inflation rate
inf_JPN = Japanese inflation rate
rypc_THD = real GDP per capita of THD
rypc_US = real GDP per capita of US
rypc_JPN = real GDP per capita of Japan
ny_THD = nominal GDP of THD
ny_US = nominal GDP of US
ny_JPN = = nominal GDP of Japan
W_IMP_THD = THD's imports from the world
W_IMP_US = US imports from the world
W_IMP_JPN = Japanese imports from the world
W_EXP_THD = THD's exports to the world
W_EXP_US = US exports to the world
W_EXP_JPN = Japanese exports to the world

# Missing Links: Regional Reforms for Asia's Bond Markets

PAUL LEJOT, DOUGLAS ARNER & LIU QIAO

## Introduction

The nature of Asia's 1997–98 crisis suggests that the region may become less prone to financial contagion by reducing reliance on its banking sectors for credit and intermediation, and improving efficiency in deploying savings. Asia is generally free from non-cyclical aggregate shortages of capital but its capability to apportion financial resources is pervasively suspect. Liquid debt securities markets exist comprehensively in no economy other than Japan, even though notes or bonds are issued in most and Asian international borrowers are well regarded, though not prolific. This article argues that active debt markets will improve national and regional resource allocation by providing an unbiased, visible price mechanism, widen the choice available to investors and diminish the contagion effects of market instability; results requiring collaborative actions that represent unprecedented economic cooperation and tests of regional and bilateral institutions. Five questions are implicit in any appraisal of the region's financial infrastructure:

- Does Asia's financial culture make mature bond markets infeasible?
- Are weak markets indicative merely of evolutionary underdevelopment?
- Can bond markets expand without continuous risk-free benchmark yield curves?

- Could new regional structures assist trading, fundraising and impaired asset resolution?
- Do potential gains in welfare justify policy engagement to strengthen Asia's bond markets?

Official interest in these issues signals a desire for financial stability. Most commentators favour active markets, although pronounced reform is unwarranted for those believing organic development sufficient for the purpose (Yoshitomi & Shirai, 2001), a view historically popular in official circles or factions that especially value bank–borrower relationships. The article describes Asia's bond markets, their roots in funding patterns, and the concerns of policymakers examining their future. It traces the origins of advanced markets, their legacy for developing economies, and suggests prescriptive lessons using research into the interplay between legal systems and financial institutions. The article concludes with proposals amenable to national interests and the nascent objectives of regional financial policy.

## Review

### Asia's Bond Markets

Asian governments have for many years issued domestic debt securities for funding or regulatory purposes but with limited participation by non-bank investors. The Philippines and Thailand were the first to issue in the 1930s; Hong Kong and Singapore only in the 1970s. Corporate debt has existed since the mid-1980s, in some cases later encouraged by partial reforms; before the Asian crisis activity was bolstered by yield-seeking offshore investors. Today's result is a family of disparate markets commonly identified as under-utilized, deficient and weak in stabilization qualities, and major currency transactions that are generally illiquid and limited in true investor participation (Arner, Lejot, Liu & Park, 2006; Crockett, 2002; Dalla & Chintakananda, 2003; Eichengreen, 1999; Harwood, 2002; Herring & Chatusripitak, 2000; McCauley, June 2003; Rhee, 2000; Yoshitomi & Shirai, 2001; and many others). No market offers reliable price continuity that provides confidence to investors or new borrowers. At first helping to intensify the Asian crisis, these weaknesses then slowed down recovery. The supply of bonds into domestic and cross-border markets has since risen but remains comparatively low. By contrast, Asia has devoted massive external surpluses to acquire highly-rated foreign assets, representing a significant post-crisis portfolio adjustment. Although non-Asian investors have partly balanced this flight of capital with risk-preferring direct investment, the trend now seems extreme and represents a loss of welfare justifiable only in the absence of appropriate institutions for crisis mitigation.

Asia's markets differ in their own fashion. Some are well developed but poorly used. Hong Kong and Singapore have effectively integrated systems but, like the unused spare wheel, their stress performance is unknown; Greenspan (2000) saw the US bond market as its economy's spare tyre, supplanting a stricken banking sector during crises. Liquidity is shallow, with only ephemeral exceptions. The quality of information offered to participants is fractured as to yields or market risks. Low-risk money market instruments are available only transiently to institutional fund managers, which decreases portfolio flexibility, deters investors and encourages contagion by denying defensive assets to those liquidating long-term investments. The markets offer no cushion against Knightian uncertainty; are poor in primary resource allocation; and only in Korea and Malaysia have recycled impaired financial assets to final investors. Bond markets are important but inessential: this encapsulates the failures of policy to achieve traction and private initiatives to become generic.

Asia lacks efficient systems, not funding. While sectoral sources of funds within each economy are non-uniform, the contribution of debt securities is far smaller and bank lending more prominent than elsewhere. Have inadequate domestic markets led to a compensating strengthening of offshore markets for Asian risk in terms of liquidity or the certainty of supply of funds? This might account for Asian risk usually commanding narrower credit spreads than suggested by relative sovereign ratings. Some Asian borrowers are internationally well established but very few maintain continuous markets in issued debt. Comparatively tight secondary conditions have prevailed for much of the last decade due to such irregular supply and the conservative stance of investors able to hold Asian risk, and thus major currency markets have only modestly compensated for intrinsically weak domestic markets.

The use of offshore sources for want of domestic liquidity has policy consequences, revealing a lack of built-in stabilizers against unforeseen volatility. It has been suggested that integration has increased within Asia's national financial sectors since the crisis, seen in Asian bank participation in international bond (and loan) transactions, and that this might prevent stress turning contagious (McCauley, Fung & Gadanecz, 2002) but the argument exaggerates the function of syndicates for distribution, rather than publicity. Moreover, syndicate size has fallen since 1994. Not all shocks are exogenous but may be provoked by herd behaviour (Borio, 2004); for example, imminent new capital requirements may have forced Japanese banks to trigger the Asian crisis, withdrawing lending from South-east Asia to avoid writing off impaired domestic assets (King, 2001). Yet transaction involvement may also indicate bank passivity or a lack of harvestable self-originated opportunities of sufficient return, and is mainly confined to deals for highly-rated borrowers. Any such integration provides no alternative intermediation and cannot lessen contagion risk without liberal last resort lending. A further hostile view is that access enjoyed by Asian issuers to offshore markets reduces incentives for local development. If a well-rated borrower's needs are fed by investment banks competing for limited transaction supply, would it encourage growth of its home bond market and compromise local bank funding? Except in Korea and Singapore, top-tier companies have promoted domestic market expansion only at the conference lectern. Similarly, banks make comparatively little use of local currency markets to raise regulatory capital: only Korean and Singaporean banks have done so in non-trivial amounts.

## Research Question

### What Makes Markets?

The bondless economy lacks market-determined interest rates to benchmark capital costs, lacks hedging instruments for risk management, restricts savers' choice and constrains institutional investment (it is less clear that borrowers in a bondless economy necessarily face higher costs of funds). It will undergo periodic banking sector strains. These circumstances describe Asia's least developed securities markets in China and Indonesia but may not imply that all economies can sustain active bond markets (Harwood, 2000: 1–37 *passim*). It has been further argued that any economy unable to borrow abroad in its own currency or borrow at home in long maturities will suffer unavoidable fragility, for all investments then entail unhedgeable currency or maturity mismatches (Eichengreen & Hausmann, 1999). The same view holds that 'older' economies became able to sell bonds offshore due to their response to significant shocks. Yet this may not be consistent: until the 1960s investment in foreign bonds was made through hubs that were home to investor groups, but there is no longer a correspondence between currency and place of issue. Market development in Asia is mainly a domestic question, for the critical need is to engage prominent home and regional investors, and large countries better attract foreign investment to their domestic issues (Bordo, Meissner & Redish, 2003): market depth is an important corollary to an economy's size.

These are grounds for market-based policy innovation, though not without cost, most immediately in improving corporate governance and regulatory enforcement. Asia's leading companies are generally able to issue public debt at home and abroad, so this is not an immediate funding problem but one of the interests of investors. For smaller companies (SMEs) that constitute most of Asia's commercial population, poor disclosure will deny access to an imposed debt market but they would be unlikely issuers even if standards were high. Indeed, this is a cause of illiquidity as important as issues of system architecture, law, taxation and investor behaviour. Natural or enhanced creditworthiness is critical to an expanded market and upon this depends the risk management benefits of bonds.

Effective bond markets require common conditions (Standard & Poor Corp., 2003):

- Strong, independent regulator of securities issuance and trading, with sound rules.
- An extended period of macroeconomic stability.
- Strong legal system and bankruptcy procedures.
- Coordinated, advanced payment, settlement, and custodial systems.
- Developed base of natural buyers of long-dated securities (pension funds and insurers).

Others look for specific indicators of sophistication while accepting that the optimal market exists only on paper (Herring & Chatusripitak, 2000). National differences in financial development may be explained by a range of factors, including legal origins, treatment of investor or property rights, or how legal systems adapt to commercial circumstances (Beck, Demirgüç-Kunt & Levine,

2002) but the inception of markets receives little attention in analysis of how financial innovation now relates to economic development.[1]

Trade in short-term government loans began in 16th century Antwerp, though the sale of public annuities in Europe dates from the late Middle Ages (van der Wee, 1977: 352 et seq.). Pools of investors willing to fund the state existed in much of the continent by the mid-17th century, most effectively in the Dutch United Provinces (Kindleberger, 1984: 156). Yet real markets existed nowhere until 1693, when Antwerp's earlier innovation of negotiability for trade bills was applied in London to the sale of the first transferable long-term government bonds. Central to their success was continual, non-arbitrary taxation, giving confidence to bondholders that future resources would service their claims, and secure creditor rights in transfer to reconcile the time horizons of debtor and creditor. Such innovation made feasible regular large-scale borrowing, and the states adopting these changes became most able to raise funds.[2]

Throughout the eighteenth and nineteenth centuries, Western governments reduced indebtedness in peacetime but borrowed without reserve when preparing for war (Ferguson, 2001). Voracious war spending demanded innovative financing; the amounts raised were of a new order to those available from any bank, state contractor or moneylender. The need to finance military spending instigated the first public debt markets (Baskin, 1988); the same markets then admitted private borrowers, initially British canal builders and US railroads (Davis & Gallman, 2001). War's inviolable demand is the root of modern debt capital markets and scale of need is crucial to their functioning. Advanced economies that built fully developed debt markets are those with a history of financing organized conflict, most beginning in the 20th century to maintain fiscal deficits for military or welfare spending (non-contributory public spending on education, employment, health or social security). Asia must establish a comparable need: the crisis and its aftermath may provide sufficient motivation and create grounds for cooperation. Output losses and the cost of supporting stricken banking sectors were enormous and an overhang of non-performing loans (NPLs) is far from removed. One year after the Asian crisis began, Hong Kong's Financial Secretary asked impassionedly, 'how is it that we in Asia have never been able to replicate the eurobond market success...?' (Tsang, 1998). He might privately have welcomed the crisis for providing sufficient incentive.

Regulatory or system arbitrage drives innovation, particularly in rule-based economies, but the growth of markets will not occur without reform, however much it may be desired by participants. Governments must legislate wherever necessary to remove or correct obstacles and inconsistencies, as well as sanctioning wholly practical elements as radical as the original US mortgage or German *Pfandbrief* markets. Does debt market development require regional impetus? There may be fears that collective action may breed non-commercial solutions or duplicate what may safely be left to the private sector. History makes it doubtful that even greatly expanded Asian economies would support liquid markets adequate for both non-bank investor activity and intermediation to militate against contagion. Indeed, certain substantial economies have never produced sophisticated debt markets. From the collapse of Bretton Woods in 1971 to the birth of the euro in 1999, France, Germany and the Netherlands maintained well developed government debt markets but elsewhere in Europe governments relied for long periods on overseas core currency issues (Belgium, Denmark, Ireland, Italy, Spain and Sweden). Except generally in Britain, robust markets for corporate debt existed only at intervals. A regional initiative in Asia appears to be essential, both to harmonize reform and give momentum to market development while respecting commercial primacy.

Government issuance must have predictability. Asian investors and intermediaries are accustomed to impromptu withdrawals of auctions or sales of notes or bonds. A similar criticism applies to multilateral organizations using Asian markets but failing to contribute liquidity with regular issues. If public borrowing is inadequate to sustain a government bond market that is liquid throughout the term structure, are fully synthetic yield curves feasible in Asian currencies, given constrained state funding? This is traditionally implausible, but synthetic yield curves can increasingly be constructed using multiple references and credit differentials. Government's role in benchmarking is central, yet synthetic instruments will gradually supplant the conventional.

More generally, practice and theory will continue to diverge. Finance theory suggests that investment is best financed by long-term capital, yet loans may have contractual features which with interest derivatives give long-term cost certainty, while options and covenants will render corporate bonds short-term or cost-uncertain. For some years in the USA and now globally, debt products have become increasingly alike. Non-bank investors trade in price-transparent loans, helped by standardization in appraisal and documentation. In developed banking markets, including parts of Asia, banking relationships are removed from decisions on asset retention, making it hazardous to identify financing tools with market segments. The widening risks covered by total return swaps and credit derivatives make this process irreversible, with inevitable consequences in times of stress, until risk appraisal improves. Product fungibility resembles the severing of the early twentieth century connection between financial centres and the currencies offered to borrowers: markets increasingly assess risks rather than the means of intermediation. Similarly, how investors distinguish credit and currency risks will affect the relationship between domestic and offshore issuance, and what is needed to promote active markets.

## Analysis

### Asia's Financing Pattern

Dependence on bank credit has roots not only in the region's relative development but in cultural flows of funds similar to those seen in Japan from the 1950s. If financial markets reflect the characteristics of underlying capital flows then Asia's bond markets may have evolved to a limited state to meet limited purposes. Conversely, it is important to consider how flows may respond to reform. Despite structural change (a general shift to managed capitalism) and great differences in per capita incomes, Asia is characterized by consistently high personal savings, recurring central fiscal surpluses or small deficits, strong recurring growth in exports and capital investment, generally low external borrowing, and intermittently favourable external balances. Since 1997 the region has collected sizeable current surpluses and international reserves, albeit not uniformly. There have been periodic exceptions after shocks, and several countries have followed distinct fiscal policies, but the region's economic characteristics are long-standing.

For 25 years, Asia's orientation has been to export promotion with fast growth in capital asset formation. The greater part of that investment has been privately sourced and deployed, with a reliance on internal funding and bank borrowing. Governments generally avoid heavy military spending and comprehensive welfare or pension schemes are typically absent. The effect of that want in encouraging precautionary savings cannot be gauged but savings ratios remain well above global averages in the few states with established provident schemes. Home ownership is far lower than in advanced economies. High savings ratios are often thought to indicate more than risk aversion and generally show no inverse correlation with per capita income. These conditions mould borrowing by companies and governments, and contribute to inefficient markets. Governments fund current spending with notes and bonds bought (willingly or otherwise) largely by banks. Often irregular, such supply cannot both fill liquidity requirements and institutional demand. Most companies are unwilling or unable to submit to new issue disclosure requirements; some are crowded out by the public sector or discriminatory regulation. Asian companies are no less rational than their foreign counterparts: internal finance is cheap when the costs associated with asymmetric information are high. The results are:

- Concentrated ownership, promoting reliance on internal funding;
- Secondary financing flows mainly from banks which militates against disclosure. Bank preferences heavily influence investment decisions;
- Bank funding depends on short-term deposits. Asia's money markets are dominated by government notes but lack the liquidity that established markets offer to non-bank participants;
- Corporate issues may require bank guarantees, irrespective of credit standing. The practice is usually induced by monopolistic banks and is unfavourable to capital market development. Credit substitution is common in China, south-east Asia and Taiwan (but will become more costly under Basel II guidelines);
- Reliance on informal debt – for example, China's banks lend sparsely to the non-state sector (Aziz & Duenwald, 2002) which instead uses internal funding, direct investment and other informal sources;[3]
- Pre-crisis growth in corporate lending by finance companies suggests banks provide inadequately for SMEs.

If active bond markets assist efficiency and welfare, is output growth impeded when they are deficient, especially since formative industrialization has long been thought to have been assisted by bank-based financial systems (Gerschenkron, 1962)? The Asian crisis resulted partly from high external debt acquisition under fixed exchange rates. Yet outside China there were few pre-1997 restrictions on domestic credit availability: this was not always inefficient. Would Asia's crisis have been milder had it been less reliant on bank intermediation? International credit lines are finite, so banks funding local lending with unhedged foreign liabilities would always have met limits. Was economic collapse inevitable after a cessation of lending? Functioning local capital markets might have encouraged a more benign outcome, providing they were sufficiently uncorrelated with bank credit activity. Systemic shocks are inevitable but the seizure that characterizes contagion is preventable: the crisis literature may neglect the contagion effects of counterparty risk (Borio, 2004).

Post-crisis changes in external capital flows may be characterized as a pause and recovery in inward foreign direct investment, a gradually diminishing flight of debt, and a substantial outflow to well-rated foreign assets. Asia's banks' most marked post-crisis action was a herd withdrawal of credit, affecting even economies least struck by losses in confidence. It prompted loan delinquency by healthy enterprises anticipating customary renewals of credit. Many banks quickly became unable to support performing assets due to losses and stronger enforcement of capital standards, some dictated by national bargains for IMF funds. Corporate loan demand duly slackened. With few low risk assets available from traditional sources, banks began to acquire non-Asian bonds, synthetic products and credit derivatives, mimicking their sponsor central banks. The core of the liquidity-sapping 'Asian bid', this may also suggest an alarming scarcity of investment opportunities.

## Discussion

### Policy Formation

Asia's needs thus represent substantial tasks for national and multilateral policy. Past regional initiatives on financial issues lacked practicality or foundered when confronted by opposing interests, for example, China, Japan or the USA, leading to doubts as to APEC's or ASEAN's competence in financial policy (Bisley, 2003; Ravenhill, 2000). Others see success in the creation of bilateral central bank repurchase and credit lines, especially their expansion following ASEAN's 2000 Chiang Mai initiative (Thomas, 2004). APEC began examining developmental ideas in 2002, including mechanisms to assist the recycling of NPLs and raise the credit quality of Asian bonds. ASEAN + 3 now sponsors similar work and the Asian Cooperation Dialogue (ASEAN + 3 plus nine Central and South Asian states) promotes political cooperation on reform. Successful outcomes would be novel: Asia's intergovernmental organizations are unused to agreeing prescriptive action on financial policy. Its trade negotiators have traditionally lacked interest, perhaps because financial services liberalization is not advanced, but this may have begun to change. Market practitioners see the post-Chiang Mai credit line framework as inconsequential, however politically important. History suggests using central bank lines only delays currency pressures. Repurchase lines established within ASEAN prior to 1997 were barely used (if at all) immediately before the crisis, due partly to a lack of collateral and to conflicts of interest. Chiang Mai's quasi-IMF conditions make credit line usage unlikely, as some participants perhaps intended.

More substantively, the Executives' Meeting of East Asia-Pacific central banks (EMEAP, comprising Australia, China, Hong Kong, Indonesia, Japan, Korea, Malaysia, New Zealand, the Philippines, Singapore and Thailand) formed in 2003 a US$1bn fund to hold core currency bonds issued by its Asian member governments. An apportionment of reserves of less than 0.1 per cent of those held by EMEAP's non-Japan Asian members, the fully-invested fund lessens liquidity but against reserve management practice includes sub-investment grade risks. The bonds held represent the fund's current investment universe. A second US$1.0bn scheme begun in 2005 involves local currency risks: families of single currency exchange traded funds and regional index funds will each hold sovereign and quasi-sovereign securities. This plan is demanding, such that it may necessitate significant cooperation on financial structure and attacks on impediments to activity. The structural concept seeks to circumvent custody, enforcement, transfer and taxation problems that exist everywhere except Hong Kong and Singapore but the plan will not directly contribute to liquidity and may contain potential conflicts of interest.[4]

## Implications and Proposals

These tentative steps suggest that specific objectives guide all national and regional reforms (ignoring standards for corporate disclosure):

- Standardize and broaden the range of available instruments as to issuers and maturities.
- Consolidate benchmarks across a declared range of maturities; introduce and adhere to visible debt issuance programmes, nationally or regionally.
- Remove trading restrictions, including repurchases of investment grade issues, short selling, and free use of interest rate and currency derivatives. Such limitations raise volatility by inducing unwarranted selling.
- Standardize clearing (real-time book entry settlement and delivery) and custody systems. Remove obstacles to securities financing to promote efficient trading and safeguard settlement liquidity. Remove barriers preventing a legal basis for trading, ownership and settlement.
- Require market-makers to provide benchmark liquidity fully visible to end users, rather than a clique of banks. Ensure that central bank operations do not lessen liquidity by relying on repurchases.
- Regulate or legislate to perfect asset and credit transfer mechanisms and rules on data retention.
- Lift regulatory restrictions arbitrarily preventing investors from acquiring debt securities, subject to purposefully harmonized credit rating floors.
- Remove, standardize or simplify withholding taxes on securities and collateral assets, and their differing applications to investor classes.
- Promote common portfolio accounting standards among banks and non-bank financial institutions.

Thus the following proposals (see Table 1) aim to promote supply and widen participation. They balance the optimal with a recognition of parochial interests and government's inevitable caution in passing authority to forces of which it may

**Table 1.** Summary of proposals

| 1 | 2 | 3 |
|---|---|---|
| Essential legal, fiscal, systemic and regulatory measures to remove identified impediments to market participation and growth, and reforms to encourage harmonization and regional usage. | A collaborative regional public debt market for domestic and major currency issues, monitored by confederal regional regulation in an established Asian financial centre. | A regional body as part of an institutional mechanism for credit enhancement to support credit risk transfer and facilitate and encourage the securitization of a wide range of assets and risks. |

be suspicious, and offer a considered means to introduce prescriptive measures. For example, Taiwan's 2002 securitization law was enacted hastily and is thought limited in use; similar questions exist of new Thai laws; EMEAP's second fund will be constrained in currency composition and freedom to invest without Proposal 1's changes, for which Proposal 2 would give momentum.

*Proposal 1*

*Remove obstacles to activity.* Active markets demand three problems be solved: intentional or implied restrictions, omissions of law or practice, and unnecessary inconsistencies within and among national domains. They exist in four categories, legal, fiscal, regulatory and systemic, forming a matrix that characterizes how issuance or investment is deterred. Table 2 uses this framework to identify where attention is most needed, particularly where common to several markets. Some features are widely known, especially since traders welcome credit and price discontinuities. The severest problems are obstacles and omissions: prices may reflect market discrepancies but legal irregularities are seldom fully compensated.

Certain legal and regulatory concerns relate to assertions of law and finance theory that legal environment, and jurisdictional or regulatory differences in investor protection are strong determinants of the effectiveness of financial systems, including capital markets, and will influence economic performance (La Porta et al. ('LLSV'), 1997 & 1998; Beck & Levine, 2003). A second thread argues that legal traditions significantly influence investor protection and market sophistication, including the view that common law traditions better support creditor rights and effective markets than civil law jurisdictions, and conversely that the protection of such rights improves the functioning of capital markets because the quality of enforcement varies with legal systems. If the nature of legal systems is a strong, timeless determinant of financial development, then market weaknesses identified in this article may be intrinsic, incapable of piecemeal remedy, and harmonized reform unable to fashion a feasible outcome.[5]

Practice will produce less rigid results. Civil law states can sustain flourishing capital markets; some common law jurisdictions do the converse. European experience since 1986 suggests that regional harmonization to minimum standards, with mutual recognition, can be effective despite varying legal and

**Table 2.** Market Impediments

| Obstacles | Omissions | Disparities |
| --- | --- | --- |
| | *Legal impediments* | |
| Qualified acceptance of ownership and property rights, and limits to such rights in relation to investor classes. | Inadequate or unreliable creditor rights in bankruptcy or reorganization, including failure of priority rights, unpredictable rules on foreclosure and status of collateral assets, and insecure priority rights after reorganizations. | Arbitrary differences in creditor status that constrain institutional investment. |
| Legal or practical barriers to the certain sale of property or financial assets, including onerous registration requirements for the transfer of claims. | Absence of clarity and consistency in settlement, custody, funds netting, securities transfer and the treatment of securities in transit. | Creditor status: uncertainty as to whether courts will enforce or dissolve private contractual creditor priorities. |
| Limits to collateral rights in bankruptcy or reorganization. | Failure to recognize trusts or equivalent insubstantive onshore or offshore entities. | Uncertainty in priority of claim and secure title. |
| Restrictive enforcement of local judgments, and inability of or refusal by courts to enforce foreign commercial judgments. | Recognition of ISDA master agreements and definitions; permissible set-off and netting in swap and derivatives contracts. | Rules on usury. |
| Limits to enforcement against public organizations; enforcement of court-sanctioned restructurings. | Custodian recognition and market admissibility of ICMA general master repurchase agreements and ISDA general collateral agreements. | Imprecision or conflicts of law. |
| Impact of exchange controls on cross-border investment, reinvestment, capital repatriation and fundraising. | | |

**Table 2.** *Continued*

| Obstacles | Omissions | Disparities |
| --- | --- | --- |
| *Fiscal impediments* | | |
| Incidence and clarity of stamp duties and other *ad valorem* taxes. | Clarity in the imposition of taxes on asset sales or the transfer of creditor claims. | Impact of withholding taxes; assessment rates, and differentials in the application of taxes and tax treaties; complexity in assessment, application, collection or exemption. |
| Duties, taxes and penalties imposed upon the transfer of financial assets and claims, and associated collateral rights. | Absence of commitments to tax neutrality for securities. | Withholding taxes and other imposts applied asymmetrically to investor groups, domiciles, instruments, coupon types or issuers. |
| Taxes and impositions that recur within single transactions, for example, in the sale of assets or claims between SPVs. | Homogeneous treatment of interest, interest deductions and accruals. | Securities financing by repurchase or lending treated as an outright sale for tax purposes. |
| Securities financing by repurchase or lending considered an outright sale for tax purposes. | Taxes imposed, applied or lifted by fiat without grandfathering, as to instruments, issuers or investor classes. | |
| *Regulatory impediments* | | |
| Prohibitions and constraints on issuers, including non-guaranteed, corporate and foreign entities. | Lack of regulatory oversight. Oversight of credit rating agencies. | Variations in rating requirements for new issues, and on minimum rating standards. |
| Regulatory restrictions on issuance and external constraints on investor activity. | Quality and reliability of mandatory issuer disclosure requirements. | Non-standardized practices by national credit rating organizations, especially when linked to regulations affecting investors. |
| Initial and current disclosure requirements and restrictions on the borrower's use of proceeds. | | An issuer's domicile may affect transaction conditions, including fiscal treatment, eligibility as collateral for repurchase agreements or permissibility in regulatory reserves. |

| | | |
|---|---|---|
| Investor constraints on permissible asset holdings and risks. | Incomplete practice framework for derivatives. | Requirements for corporate debt issues to be guaranteed by third party financial institutions. |
| Ease of establishing and operating foreign owned investment funds. | | |
| Responsibility divided between competing regulators. | | |
| Unpredictable political reviews of judicial decisions. | | |

*Systemic impediments*

| | | |
|---|---|---|
| Limits on access to money market, short-term or other eligible instruments. | Absence of declared or consistent benchmark issuance programmes. | Government issue primary dealer qualifications, requirements and exclusions. |
| Restrictions on settlement or custody. | Transparent and declared objectives for monetary policy. | Variations in settlement practice; settlement risks (lack of book entry operations, real-time settlement and reporting). |
| Prohibitions on securities lending and short-sales. | Coordination between national debt management strategy and monetary policy. | Rules on custody for domestic and foreign investors. |
| General illiquidity. | Availability and price transparency of interest rate swaps and other hedging products | Elective use of central depositaries for settlement or custody and elective physical delivery of bond certificates. |
| Inequitable qualifications or restrictions on dealing. | Poor settlement practices and associated risks in settlement. | Delivery against payment not applied consistently across instruments or classes of issuer. |

institutional settings. Harmonized reform is valuable despite obstacles that make common objectives achievable only in different ways – the greatest benefit of a successful EMEAP local currency fund. Joint efforts show purpose to market participants; resource sharing is efficient despite national differences in systems; and collective action will nurture intra-regional local currency investment. The EU's 1987 Single European Act sought to liberate capital movement by subsidiarity, providing minimum standards for implementation through national legislation that differed among those signing the Act (1987 OJ (L169) 1 (1987)). Except in Britain, an absence of securities market legislation generally meant that few obstacles to harmonization first needed removal (Arner, 2002), and the remaining obstacles are being addressed by the European Securities Committee and Committee of European Securities Regulators. Mutual recognition became the second stage of reform. Asia's governments would agree common intentions and then each implement appropriate mechanics to address the problems shown in Table 2, noting that, 'the evolution of the legal framework underlying efficient market economies was a long incremental process (...). If the legal framework does not already exist or only partially exists it must be created.' (North, 1995: 11).

### Proposal 2

*Regional hub market.*  Reforms could be hastened by governments sanctioning a regulated market for regional, domestic and non-Asian use. From an agreed date, the trading and settlement of new and outstanding bonds would be permitted in a hub that meets agreed standards, free of withholdings, duties and capital controls, subject to common regulation and available to all investors and approved issuers. This would remove confusion, relieve delays and provide confidence to participants. Alternatively, the model could begin the construction of an integrated regional multi-currency debt market. The (pre-euro) eurobond markets were a successful precedent, except that participating countries would not restrict new issues in an obligor's home currency as in France and Italy until the 1980s, since one objective is to meld the interests of domestic and offshore investors. With national agreement made, new issues would be launched and traded in the offshore centre. Domestic participants would deal through the centre's systems, although retail investors would use domestic intermediaries to assist investor protection. The proposal requires four undertakings:

- Participating governments lift restrictions and regulations that may limit or prohibit investing and trading in the hub by financial institutions and intermediaries for which they are responsible.
- The host government allows the expanded market to develop unhindered, and agrees not to impose restrictions or penalties on investment activity or payments other than sanctioned by the competent regulatory authority to which participating governments would subscribe. The host authorities undertake to maintain agreed standards for market practice.
- The host authority from inception becomes subject to observation by an advisory council in which all participating governments are represented,

but shall itself have day-to-day supervision of settlement and securities custody.

• Participating governments maintain allegiance to the concept for a defined period of an initial ten years, with retroactive coverage preventing the withdrawal of consents during the life of issues created during that period.

The first undertaking is fundamental, requiring modest legal and regulatory changes in domestic jurisdictions. The second requires consensus on standards for market practice and access, for which both international efforts and the problems identified in Table 2 are guides (Goo, Arner & Zhou, 2001). The hub will have met the required standards when chosen. The third demands cooperation among national governments and represents compensation for perceived sacrifices of parochial interest. The final undertaking relates to confidence and its effect on activity: this will also concern regional negotiations on trade in financial services.

The proposal requires national efforts in detailed aspects of law or its application, and regional agreement in sharing costs for Asia's collective welfare. Critically, it requires no new systems and only minor institutional arrangements. In assimilating the prescriptions of Proposal 1 it would provide a spur to a regional debt market, building on existing national practices without affecting them deleteriously. The proposal assumes that choice of location is unimportant for most financial market activities, given accepted regulatory and system requirements. Nearly all trading is electronic, and business days among EMEAP members are almost contiguous. Using one hub for trading and settlement would stimulate investor activity, including regional and other international flows that are now neglected for want of simple infrastructure and procedures. Trade flows and streams of direct or portfolio investment generate natural demand for short and long-term debt instruments, hedging products and tools to assist capital asset benchmarking. Momentum will grow from identified but untapped regional sources rather than an increase in the core of demand now emanating from commercial banks and risk traders, although an expansion in volume can be expected from domestic professional participants trading through the hub. Last, the market would facilitate syndication of domestic government debt as an alternative to auctions, immediately raising liquidity and investor interest. The plan involves no patrician losses for national governments and no elimination of present systems. This 'offshore' market need be in no sense unregulated.

Participating governments will allow fungible trading by domestic and offshore participants. The key matters for pre-commencement decision are regulatory capacity, settlement capacity in the hub clearing vehicle and for direct or indirect custody, uniform settlement conditions, and a commitment to minimize settlement days. The hub's exchange listing requirements would not be changed by this proposal, except if required for admission of issues originating in participating countries, especially in relation to credit ratings or jurisdiction of incorporation. Listings are sought by custom and provide links to regulatory supervision of reporting and disclosure but are not associated with trading or price information. There need be no ceding of responsibility between national authorities: a harmonized approach employing common standards underpins the hub concept, with approvals where necessary to be given as now. In each phase of a transaction, operations are managed in the offshore market to promote price transparency, maximize secondary liquidity by combining domestic and offshore trading, and exploit scale economies in unified electronic systems. Trades between counterparties in the issuer's domicile would be reported centrally and settled through the offshore market. This also removes uncertainty arising from the choice of law or jurisdiction in cross-border disputes by having the location of settlement and custody determine organically the law to which securities in settlement or custody are subject. The hub authorities could also adopt an international convention further to support investor confidence: the leading example is the Hague Convention No. 36 on the law applicable to certain rights in respect of securities held with an intermediary, part of the Hague Conference on Private International Law.

In these respects the proposal mimics the eurobond market of the late 1980s and early 1990s. If domestic and offshore investors buy a new issue then both proceeds and bonds will be fungible, although for convenience separate temporary 'notes' could be lodged electronically representing domestic and offshore tranches; the size of each tranche will vary after payment. The political component of credit risk is thus no different for investors to that which they accept today, except that domestic investors will assume negligible risks against the hub clearing house, as with all international settlement institutions. Legal risks arising from a withdrawal of national concessions are unaltered. Creditor claims will be treated no differently from today for most bond issues convey no direct collateral rights. Providing that borrowers enter transaction agreements written under governing laws acceptable to listing authorities approved by the hub's regulator then applications for judgments or enforcement would be conducted as disparately as today. Domestic investors would not be prejudiced in their traditional choice of law in cases where market practice is well established, but issuers are certain to be required to submit to non-exclusive jurisdiction in generally accepted international forums, and could expect a pricing disincentive compared with 'standard' hub issues as adequate enforcement of judgments is central to Proposal 1. Last, for government debt only, a conservative alternative proposal would leave primacy of hub trading and settlement with domestic institutions but allow unhindered foreign investor participation through a single channel for settlement and custody. This resembles EMEAP's local currency fund. Hub banks would not be restricted in accepting deposits in hub issue currencies.

Proposal 2 builds on acceptance of hub regulatory standards (embodying agreed practice) rather than harmonization as in the implied objectives of Proposal 1. It is a market-orientated way of dealing with impediments and non-uniform practice and requires little legislation or regulatory change providing that liquidity is allowed in conventional currency derivatives. It is far simpler than proposals for single, hub or basket currencies intended to lessen exchange volatility (Frankel, 2003: 44) and, if political goals are agreed, represents a practical first step in creating a framework for long-term regional stability. It carries none of the unknown costs of new or hybrid currencies, nor requires the removal of market segmentation by currency that might endanger the development of Asian banks. While the early life of the euro has greatly increased issuance in the European corporate debt markets, the removal of entry barriers of legacy currency sectors allowed a huge increase in the market share of global underwriters. Distribution skills may outweigh client relationships for banks seeking bond transactions (Santos & Tsatsaronis, 2003: 14). Nonetheless, if currency cooperation becomes an explicit policy objective then Proposal 2's hub and Proposal 1's key reforms would together facilitate market integration, and contribute to the introduction of new foreign exchange regimes.

## *Proposal 3*

*Credit enhancement.* A new credit enhancement agency will help recycle by securitization the accumulation of impaired assets in Asia's banking systems. This would yield a flow of well-rated securities and bequeath a standardized mechanism appropriate for most aspects of credit risk transfer, and later assist infrastructural fund raising and improve the provision of credit for SMEs. The proposal requires a suitably capitalized vehicle to encourage risk-pooling, credit risk transfer, rating-targeting and in particular to provide a new source of external transactional credit enhancement. It includes no formal limitation on source credit risk, whilst instruments of issue might include all conventional and hybrid term debt securities, and structured money market instruments such as asset-backed commercial paper. The plan is ambitious but specific in its application of resources. It requires national endorsement, regional cooperation and a resource commitment, partly in funded equity but largely by means of cost-effective contingent capital, that is, a contractual, irrevocable commitment to fund an infusion of equity according to pre-determined criteria.

Securitization is the irrevocable transfer of defined financial assets by their originator, with consideration funded by the simultaneous sale to a third party of securities issued by the asset buyer. Neither buyer nor investor has transactional recourse to the originator. The buyer is an insubstantive vehicle (company or trust). Most securitized transactions use internal or external credit enhancement to ensure the securities achieve target credit ratings. Internal enhancement usually takes the form of over-collateralization or a liquidity reserve; external enhancement is commonly cash collateral, third-party financial guarantees (US standby letters of credit) or insurance. Securities are typically issued in tiers carrying different commercial terms and risks to maximize the use of assets and associated cash flows.

This article does not consider wholly synthetic issues, which apply credit derivatives to asset portfolios that then remain on the balance sheet of the originator. Proposal 3 must also be distinguished from other distinct instruments. For example, holders of US federal agency bonds generally acquire indirect interests in financial assets purchased by the issuer without rights of enforcement against those assets. Buyers of European covered bonds acquire preferred interests in assets that change in composition and remain on the balance sheet of the originator-issuer. An Asian covered bond market could be created using the ratings of a multilateral institution, mirroring a concept under discussion in the EU. Both US agency and German *Pfandbriefe* markets were founded with state backing and utilize indirect sovereign credit.

Common to all securitized transactions is adequate enhancement of the credit risk offered to investors by the manipulation or augmentation of underlying source assets, be they a whole business, similar but unconnected assets or streams of cash, and circumvent problems of weak corporate credit or disclosure. There are five ways in which the process becomes manifest, and these are the proposal's central aims:

- Generally, the means to make an unacceptable risk satisfactory to an investor.
- An overt or implied credit rating better than its respective sovereign ceiling.
- The means to price unvalued pools of assets (usually to make feasible their sale).
- A method to create capital market funding where none previously existed.
- For originators, a funding source where none was available at an acceptable cost.

Unpredictability harshly affects the economics of structured transactions. The marginal cost of an inaugural deal is justified if it heralds a series: too often this has proved impossible for lack of suitable material or by the obstruction of law. The post-crisis imperative for balance sheet repair made transaction costs more tolerable, resulting in a notable shift in assets, a growth in synthetic transactions since 1999–2000 and an improvement in bank and corporate balance sheets in certain countries, notably Korea and Malaysia. Proposal 3 is a logical further step to accelerate the recycling of non-accruing or delinquent financial assets, which when established assists the transparent sale-pricing of NPLs: market-clearing yields on new securities determine the permissible sale price of collateral asset pools. Moreover, it will add to Asia's feasible issuers by providing banks with explicit risk support for a refinancing mechanism to encourage competitive lending for risks of lesser quality, free of sovereign rating ceilings.

By facilitating structured finance on a regional scale to deal with the continuing problem of recognized, undeclared or unpriced impaired assets, Asia's governments will allow future growth in capital market activity and offer reliable supply of debt instruments to institutional investors. The transaction framework is well understood:

- Financial assets are sold by their originator to a domestic trust, then resold to an offshore trust that funds the purchase, simultaneously or after a period for asset accumulation, with an array of new securities enjoying direct claims of varying seniority over all or part of the asset pool.
- Qualifying assets are chosen by transaction feasibility, and include impaired assets, commercial mortgage loans, corporate loans and major lease receivables. Asset servicing becomes independent of the originator. The originator may continue to deal commercially with any ultimate debtor except in cases involving impaired assets.
- Debt securities are issued in tranches, designed commercially and by priority to meet investor preferences while extracting the fullest value from pool cash or proceeds.

- Credit enhancement is given by a new regional organization incorporated in a tax neutral jurisdiction and managed in an Asian financial centre. Shareholder capital will be provided by governments, international financial organizations and perhaps a minority of private institutions. The official shareholders will form a supervisory body responsible for general regulatory matters.
- External sources provide such additional credit support that each series of bonds meets target credit ratings. This backing is given by a third party through funded or contingent capital, financial guarantee or insurance. It may cover defaults within a collateral pool, whole transactions or support swap collateralization.

Structured finance is the complex achieving the simple, in this case a supply of new issues with superior credit ratings. Asia has hosted many structured issues since 1997–98, usually supported by blanket guarantees (for example, Hong Kong Mortgage Corporation issues) or foreign monoline insurer wraps but Asia's only indigenous monoline collapsed after the crisis: Asian Securitization & Infrastructure Assurance (Pte) Limited ('ASIA Ltd'), formed in 1996, was poorly capitalized and so carried a single-A rating inadequate for feasible credit enhancement. ASIA Ltd may have needed US$700 million in founding capital to obtain AAA ratings (Hong Kong Monetary Authority research cited in Dalla, 2002).

In contrast, this proposal's innovation springs from cost-effectiveness and productive scope in external credit enhancement, how new (non-distressed) financial assets are volunteered for securitization, and its regional administration. Resources will be applied predominantly to the provision of transactional or programme credit enhancement, ideally with administration and risk management outsourced as with Euroclear prior to 2001. The proposal offers a continuing means to generate securities of credit quality acceptable to investors, using hitherto unsuitable assets (in addition to NPLs). Proposal 3 would give such continuity of supply that investors see structured finance as predictable rather than episodic. It anticipates a shift in rating practice such that seasoned asset-backed bonds (ABSs) are subject to periodic review to reflect the maturing of asset pools and phased redemption of securities. A contingent capital structure is well-suited to this approach. For each transaction given credit enhancement, a provision of funded capital would be assigned at launch, together with an unconditional commitment to supplement that funded contribution if certain events occur.

Banks can be effective providers of finance for medium-scale enterprises (they are accustomed to imperfect information and high initial lending costs) but may need incentives to lend, not only at times of heightened risk. SME issuance will remain largely infeasible. The relaxation after 1987 of US Glass–Steagall legislation allowing commercial banks to underwrite corporate securities led initially to their arranging a disproportionate number of modest issues for SMEs partly due to the competitive power of investment banks (Gande, Puri, Saunders & Walker, 1997). The reform improved SME funding, and shows the value of SME lenders developing capital market skills. Proposal 3 would embrace all financial assets and cause a considerable increase in issuance without disturbing bank–SME relationships. The concept resembles that used after 1999 to recycle defaulted or delinquent Korean bonds and NPLs (Oh, Park, Park & Yang, 2003). For investors, the agency provides access to credit risk more complete and transparent than generally available. The proposal only relates to portfolio change, not to altering the credit characteristics of single obligor risks: transactions or derivatives based on such risks would be left wholly to the private sector. Ignoring co-financing, international organizations have given single obligor guarantees in stress conditions. No such transaction has created a favourable precedent; all were costly models. The main considerations of the proposal are inherent costs, essential regional cooperation, and the removal of obstacles described in Proposal 1, especially in achieving price transparency in asset sales. ABS issues are no less demanding than corporate bonds in accounting or legal questions, and (as with sophisticated markets) the proposal may not work universally with equal effect. When accepted nationally, Basel II's accord has implications for some transactions supported by this proposal but would not make a material difference to its effectiveness.

## Conclusion

These proposals are not mutually exclusive. The simplest means to remove obstacles to development (Proposal 1) is to permit a collaborative offshore market for which from inception no impediment can exist (2), as seen elsewhere, 'The rapid emergence in the 1960s of a worldwide Eurocurrency market (...) resulted from the peculiarly stringent and detailed official regulations governing residents operating with their own national currencies.' (McKinnon, 1977: 2). Second, permitting an offshore market will facilitate the speedy introduction of more complex mechanisms to allow securitization on the broadest scale (3), even without legal changes. Active markets will exist only with governmental commitment to reform, providing all commitments are market orientated. These proposals favour open price mechanisms in an institutional sense and should not be taken as suggesting that bank-centred or market-centred systems are intrinsically superior, nor that the means by which financial sector reform is introduced can be universal.

## Acknowledgements

The authors acknowledge the comments provided by two anonymous referees and the support of the Hong Kong Institute for Monetary Research, the University of Hong Kong's Research Initiation Grant programme and the Hong Kong Research Grants Council Competitive Earmarked Research Grant programme.

### Notes

[1] Taking Hicks's view (1969) that financial development precedes and stimulates growth, it is reasonable to identify prominent exogeneities associated with market development. In the long-run growth may influence an economy's 'institutional framework' (North, 1995: 2); Gurley & Shaw (1955) argue that the 'development of financial institutions (...) is both a determined and a determining variable in the growth process'. Otherwise, no contemporary body of theory holds that primary causation flows from growth to finance. Robinson's statement 'enterprise leads finance' (1953: 86) is taken literally (Levine, 1997; Rousseau & Sylla, 2001; Fase, 2003) but was unrelated to financial markets; the nature of

'finance' is entirely a current debate. The substantial work postulating strong casual links between financial and economic development (from Goldsmith, 1969; Shaw, 1973; to King & Levine, 1993) is not unquestioned, for example, empirically (Favara, 2003) or qualitatively, especially for using partial liquidity or credit as proxies for systemic development.

[2] Some argue that Spain's Dutch provinces developed the first 'permanent public debt market' (Rousseau & Sylla, 2001) but van der Wee (1977) shows that the trade was confined to short-term public finance loans: annuities were cumbersome to transfer. Antwerp invented negotiable trade bills by 1547 but failed to apply similar principles to create a long-term public debt market (ibid., p.323 ff.), and may thus have ceded leadership in financial securities to London. Dickson (1967: 457) shows that England's 'financial revolution' after 1688 made possible a public bond market, the absence of which 'would have effectively stopped (the state) from borrowing on the scale it needed'. The 1689 Bill of Rights is to North (1991: 101) an essential change: 'A capital market (...) will simply not evolve where political rulers can arbitrarily seize assets or radically alter their value.' These problems persist in post-crisis Asia.

[3] Including 'effective, non-standard financing channels' (Allen, Qian & Qian, 2002: 4–5) (suggesting equivalents in other economies) and 'privately placed bonds and loans' (ibid: 32),. Recent research indicates that revenue and income profit disguising is widespread and an effective external source of funds (Cai et al, 2004; Liu & Lu, 2004; Liu and Xiao, 2004; Xiao, 2004). Much foreign investment may be loans, disguised to avoid exchange controls (Fernald & Babson, 1999; Xiao, 2004). More generally, the use of external finance may not be a function of available choice but ultimately of firm size (Beck, Demirgüç-Kunt, & Maksimovic, 2002).

[4] Central banks are privileged investors in that they regulate and dominate domestic activity and influence issuance. Although EMEAP's administration is outsourced it would be unrealistic to expect full portfolio disclosure or a separation of interests that might compromise established central bank operations (Lejot & Arner, 2004).

[5] Aspects of law and finance theory are difficult to test. Creditor data are erratic (equity claims are simpler to identify); the determined variable 'debt' is commonly taken as the sum of bank claims against the non-banking sector and disclosed or public non-financial bond issues (LLSV, 1997, 1998 and may exaggerate sophistication in bank-based systems. It may also confuse aspects of rights relating to the enforcement of collateral since (except in the USA) a higher proportion of bank claims are secured than those of bondholders. Data weaknesses erode the view that the treatment of claims denotes effective markets. 'Financial development' often fails to distinguish between the availability of or growth in credit, and the sophistication of the system. Empirical problems in assessing comparative creditor rights suggest that the theory intrinsically uses a common law perspective. The scale of bank assets (LLSV, 1997) cannot alone signal sophistication in Asian markets (anticipated by Goldsmith, 1969) for bank cartels are widespread; large companies may borrow in all environments, at home or abroad (acknowledged by LLSV, 1997: 1148). Further, certain analyses aggregate debt and equity claims, despite differences in their respective rights and agency problems being associated mainly with equity claims. Eichengreen & Luengnaruemitchai (2004) and Burger & Warnock (2004) respectively examine the determinants of bond market capitalization in Asia and in up to 49 local markets. Both concur with LLSV that country size, growth, creditor rights and certain risk factors are important determinants of market size, but the former find Asia's lack of large markets suggests conservative fiscal policies and cultural factors. Each acknowledge data limitations, not least in identifying reverse causality.

# References

Allen, F., Qian, Jun & Qian, Meijun (2002) Law Finance and Economic Growth in China, Wharton Financial Institutions Center, working paper 0244.

Arner, D. (2002) Globalization of financial markets: an international passport for securities offerings?, *International Lawyer*, 35, pp. 1543–1588.

Arner, D., Lejot, P., Liu, Q. & Park, J-H. (2006) *Asia's Debt Capital Markets: Prospects and Strategies for Development* (Santa Monica, CA: Milken Institute/Springer).

Aziz, J. & Duenwald, C. (2002) Growth–Financial Intermediation Nexus in China, IMF, working paper 02/194.

Baskin, J. (1988) The development of corporate financial markets in Britain and the United States, 1600–1914: overcoming asymmetric information, *Business History Review*, 62(2), pp. 199–237.

Beck, T., Demirgüç-Kunt, A. & Levine, R. (2002) Law and Finance: Why does Legal Origin Matter?, World Bank policy research, working paper 2904.

Beck, T., Demirgüç-Kunt, A. & Maksimovic, V. (2002) Financing Patterns around the World: the Role of Institutions, World Bank policy research, working paper 2905.

Beck, T. & Levine, R. (2003) Legal Institutions and Financial Development, National Bureau of Economic Research, working paper 10126.

Bisley, N. (2003) The end of East Asian regionalism?, *Journal of East Asian Affairs*, (XVII)1), pp. 148–171.

Bordo, M., Meissner, C. & Redish, A. (2003) How Original Sin was Overcome: the Evolution of External Debt Denominated in Domestic Currencies in the United States and the British Dominions 1800–2000, National Bureau of Economic Research, working paper 9841.

Borio, C. (2004) Market Distress and Vanishing Liquidity: Anatomy and Policy Options, BIS working paper 158

Burger, J. & Warnock, F. (2004) Foreign Participation in Local Currency Bond Markets, Federal Reserve System, international finance discussion papers 794.

Cai, Hongbin, Liu, Qiao & Xiao, Geng (2004) Does Competition Discipline Firms? The Case of Corporate Profit Hiding in China, Hong Kong Institute of Economics and Business Strategy working paper 1126.

Crockett, A. (2002) Capital Flows in East Asia Since the Crisis, speech in Beijing to ASEAN+3 group, BIS, October.

Dalla, I. (2002) Asset-backed Securities Markets in Selected East Asian Countries, mimeo, World Bank.

Dalla, I. & Chintakananda, A. (2003) Harmonization of Bond Market Rules and Regulations, Background Study for APEC Finance Ministers Process, Asian Development Bank.

Davis, L. & Gallman, R. (2001) *Evolving Financial Markets and International Capital Flows: Britain, the Americas, and Australia, 1865–1914*, pp. 35–36 (Cambridge: Cambridge University Press).

Dickson, P. (1967) *The Financial Revolution in England: A Study in the Development of Public Credit 1688–1756* (London: Macmillan).

Eichengreen, B. (1999) Toward a New International Financial Architecture: a Practical Post-Asia Agenda, Institute for International Economics.

Eichengreen, B. & Hausmann, R. (1999) Exchange Rates and Financial Fragility, National Bureau of Economic Research working paper 7418.

Eichengreen, B. & Luengnaruemitchai, P. (2004) Why Doesn't Asia have Bigger Bond Markets?, National Bureau of Economic Research working paper 10576.

Fase, M. (2003) Financial Environment and Economic Growth in Selected Asian Countries, *Journal of Asian Economics*, 14, pp. 11–21.

Favara, G. (2003) An Empirical Reassessment of the Relationship between Finance and Growth, IMF working paper 03/123.

Fernald, J. & Babson, O. (1999) Why has China Survived the Asian Crisis so Well? What Risks Remain?, Federal Reserve System international finance discussion papers 633.

Ferguson, N. (2001) *The Cash Nexus: Money and Power in the Modern World 1700–2000* (London: Basic Books).

Frankel, J. (2003) Experience of and Lessons from Exchange Rate Regimes in Emerging Economies, John F. Kennedy School of Government, Harvard University, working paper 03011.

Gande, A., Puri, M., Saunders, A. & Walker, I. (1997) Bank Underwriting of Securities: Modern Evidence, *Review of Financial Studies*, 10(4), pp. 1175–1202.

Gerschenkron, A. (1962) Reflections on the Concept of 'Prerequisites' of Modern Industrialization in A. Gerschenkron, *Economic Backwardness in Historical Perspective* (Cambridge MA: Belknap Press).

Goo, S., Arner, D. & Zhou, Z. (Eds) (2001) *International Financial Sector Reform: Standard Setting and Infrastructure Development* (London: Kluwer).

Goldsmith, R. (1969) *Financial Structure and Development* (New Haven CT: Yale University Press).

Greenspan, A. (2000) Global Challenges, speech to Financial Crisis Conference, Council on Foreign Relations.

Gurley, J. & Shaw, E. (1955) Financial Aspects of Economic Development, *American Economic Review*, 45(4), pp. 515–538.

Harwood, A. (Ed.) (2000) *Building Local Bond Markets, An Asian Perspective*, International Finance Corporation.

Harwood, A. (Ed.) (2002) Building Corporate Bond Markets in Emerging Market Countries, presentation to OECD/ World Bank workshop on bond markets.

Herring, R. & Chatusripitak, N. (2000) The Case of the Missing Market: the Bond Market and why it Matters for Financial Development, Asian Development Bank Institute working paper.

Hicks, J. (1969) *Theory of Economic History* (Oxford: Clarendon Press).

Kindleberger, C. (1984) *A Financial History of Western Europe* (New York: Oxford, University Press).

King, M. (2001) Who triggered the Asian financial crisis?, *Review of International Political Economy*, 8(3), pp. 438–466.

King, R. & Levine, R. (1993) Finance and Growth: Schumpeter Might be Right, *Quarterly Journal of Economics*, 108(3), pp. 717–737.

La Porta, R., López-de-Silanes, F., Shleifer, A. & Vishny, R. (1997) Legal Determinants of External Finance, *Journal of Finance*, 52(3), pp. 1131–1150.

La Porta, R., López-de-Silanes, F., Shleifer, A. & Vishny, R. (1998) Law and Finance, *Journal of Political Economy*, 106(6), pp. 1113–1155.

Lejot, P. & Arner, P. (2004) Well-intentioned Asian Bond Fund won't Work, *International Financial Law Review*, 23(9), pp. 54–57.

Levine, R. (1997) Financial Development and Economic Growth: Views and Agenda, *Journal of Economic Literature*, 35(2), pp. 688–726.

Liu, Qiao & Lu, Zhou (2004) Earnings Management to Tunnel: Evidence from China's Listed Companies, Hong Kong Institute of Economics and Business Strategy working paper 1097.

Liu, Qiao & Xiao, Geng (2004) Look Who Are Disguising Profits: An Application to Chinese Industrial Firms, Hong Kong Institute of Economics and Business Strategy working paper 1095.

McCauley, R. (2003) Capital Flows in East Asia Since the 1997 Crisis, *BIS Quarterly Review*, June, pp. 41–56.

McCauley, R., Fung, S. S. & Gadanecz, B. (2002) Integrating the finances of East Asia, *BIS Quarterly Review*, Dec, pp. 83–96.

McKinnon, R. (1977) *The Eurocurrency Market*, Essays on International Finance 125, Princeton.

North, D. (1991) Institutions, *Journal of Economic Perspectives*, 5(1), pp. 97–112.

North, D. (1995) Some Fundamental Puzzles in Economic History/Development, Economics Working Paper Archive at WUSTL No. 9509001.

Oh, G. T., Park, D. K., Park, J. H. & Yang, D. Y. (2003) How to Mobilize the Asian Savings within the Region: Securitization and Credit Enhancement for the Development of East Asia's Bond Market, Korea Institute for International Economic Policy working paper 03–02, Seoul.

Ravenhill, J. (2000) APEC Adrift: Implications for Economic Regionalism in Asia and the Pacific, *Pacific Review*, 13(2), pp. 319–333.

Rhee, S. G. (2000) Rising to Asia s Challenge: Enhanced Role of Capital Markets, in, *Rising to the Challenge in Asia: A Study of Financial Markets*, Vol.1, Asian Development Bank.

Robinson, J. (1953) *The Rate of Interest and Other Essays* (London: Macmillan).

Rousseau, P. & Sylla, R. (2001) Financial Systems, Economic Growth and Globalization, National Bureau of Economic Research working paper 8323.

Santos, J. & Tsatsaronis, K. (2003) The Cost of Barriers to Entry: Evidence from the Market for Corporate Euro Bond Underwriting, BIS working paper 134

Shaw, E. (1973) *Financial Deepening in Economic Development* (New York: Oxford).

Standard and Poor's Corporation (2003) How Domestic Capital Markets can help Sovereign Creditworthiness (New York: Standard and Poor).

Thomas, N. (2004) An East Asian Economic Community: Multilateralism Beyond APEC Presentation to Asia-Pacific Economies: Multilateral vs. Bilateral Relationships Conference, City University of Hong Kong, May 2004, available at http://www.cityu.edu.hk/cityu/events/APBC.htm (accessed 13 April 2006).

Tsang, D. (1998) Financial secretary's speech at Asian Debt Conference, 6 July 1998, available at http://info.gov.hk/gia/general/199807/06/0706078. htm (accessed 13 April 2006).

Van der Wee, H. (1977) Monetary, Credit and Banking Systems, in: E. Rich & C. Wilson (Eds) *The Cambridge Economic History of Europe; V, Economic Organization of Early Modern Europe* (Cambridge: Cambridge University Press).

Xiao, Geng (2004) People's Republic of China's Round-tripping FDI: Scale, Causes and Implications, Manila, Asian Development Bank Institute discussion paper No.7.

Yoshitomi, M. & Shirai, S. (2001) Designing a Financial Market Structure in Post-Crisis Asia; How to Develop Corporate Bond Markets, Asian Development Bank Institute working paper 15.

# Stimulating Private Sector Development in China: The Emergence of Enterprise Development Centres in Liaoning and Sichuan Provinces

ANDREW ATHERTON & ALARIC FAIRBANKS

The emergence of the private sector is beginning to change the profile and dynamics of the Chinese economy, including its institutional framework (*Asia Monitor*, 2003; Dickson, 2003; Gregory & Tenev, 2001; Li and Rozelle, 2003; Oi, 1995; Tsai, 2002; Wang, 2004; Wiemer and Tian, 2001). Historical dependence on state-owned enterprises and latterly on public–private partnerships in the ownership and management of township and village enterprises appears to be decreasing as the private economy grows (Cooke, 2005; *The Economist*, 2000), and as ownership structures are being reformed; for example by addressing the tendency for some private businesses to wear the 'red hat' of collective ownership (e.g. Tsai, 2002: 130). Garnaut *et al.* (2001) have described these changes in ownership as China's 'quiet revolution' and the third major institutional transformation of the reform period.

Parallel to private sector growth has been increased public policy recognition of the importance of small and medium enterprises (SMEs)[1] to future economic development. The SME Promotion Law, published in 2003, states that government has a role to play in supporting, stimulating and enabling the development and growth of smaller private enterprises, because smaller businesses will contribute increasingly to employment and wealth creation in the future. The Law requires municipalities and local governments to establish SME support systems and to integrate support for enterprises into their local economic development plans and strategies.

This article analyses one aspect of local SME support systems, namely the creation of specialist institutions dedicated to enterprise development. It examines the emergence of small and medium enterprise development and advice centres in six cities in the provinces of Liaoning in the north-east and Sichuan in the south-west.[2] The article examines the contexts within which the centres were established, and explores the factors that contributed to their development.

## Development of the Private Sector in China

The growth of the private sector in China is one of several dimensions of the restructuring and reform of the economy away from a planned system to a 'socialist market economy' (Wang, 2004) and a 'market economy with Chinese characteristics' (Hughes, 2002). These changes and reforms have occurred since Deng Xiaoping came to power in 1978 and represent a consistent approach to economic policy across successive leaderships (Nathan and Gilley, 2003). Indeed, a characteristic of China's development has been the role of government in gradually encouraging reform (Propopenko, 2004) and alternative approaches to economic development policy (Nolan, 2004).

The emergence of Township and Village Enterprises (TVEs) represented a major change in the structure of the domestic Chinese economy. These enterprises generated significant growth in rural areas through the second half of the 1980s and into the 1990s (e.g. Tong, 2001). In a similar pattern to reforms in agriculture (c.f. Ash, 1988), the principles of public ownership and private management, typically via contracting arrangements, underpinned these enterprises. This led to a distinctive form of Chinese business and economic ownership and management where government officials, typically at the local level, operated as coordinators and enablers of privately managed but publicly owned businesses (Gibb & Li, 2003; Kwong & Lee, 2000; Unger & Chan, 1999). As the rapid growth of TVEs was slowing in the second half of the 1990s (Li & Rozelle, 2003; Nolan 2004: 12), local governments attempted to address falling rates of growth and increasing levels of under-performance via a variety of mechanisms and strategies, often focusing around changes in ownership structure (e.g. Sun, 2000).

Reform of the state-owned enterprise sector has also led to changes in ownership from public to private. As industrial policy focused on the formation of China's 'national champions', i.e. large and very large corporations that the government believed could compete in global markets (Nolan, 2004), medium and small enterprises were released from public ownership. A policy of 'holding on to the large and releasing the small' (*zhuada fangxiao*) emerged, leading to the transfer of many smaller state-owned enterprises to the private sector (Hughes, 2002).

As well as growth in the private sector through changes in ownership, there has been encouragement of self-employment and small-scale enterprise since the early days of the post-Mao reform period (Wang, 2004). Legislation to recognize and support self-employment was introduced in 1981, allowing individuals to set up *getihu* (literally single person establishments), and was followed in 1998 by legal recognition of private enterprises (Gold, 1991: 157–180; Lau *et al.*, 1999). These businesses were subject to minimal formal regulation by the state, although ad hoc taxation and other forms of government charging were and continue to be rife (ibid.; Tsai, 2002; Tsang, 1994). As Lau *et al.* (1999: 38) noted, private businesses face an uncertain relationship with the state: '…private entrepreneurs still fear the loss of their private property in case of political backlash. They thus hesitate to invest too much in their businesses under the threat of the "fat pig policy", a situation in which the state waits until businesses have become sizeable and then takes them over.'

## The Case for Supporting Private Sector Development in China

Support for the development of private sector small and medium enterprises is intrinsic to industrial policy in all developed economies (e.g. DTI, 2001; EC, 2003; METI, 2002; OECD, 1998), and can be seen as an important focus of economic development and poverty reduction policies and frameworks in emerging and transition economies (e.g. Bear *et al.*, 2004; World Bank, 2001). In most developing countries, smaller enterprises generate a significant share of private sector economic activity and are seen as fundamental to poverty reduction and economic growth (World Bank, 2002). Successive studies have established that small firms generate the majority of new jobs in many developed nations (Birch, 1979; Broesma & Gautier, 1997; Gallagher *et al.*, 1991; Heshmati, 2001; Hohti, 2000; Konings, 1995; Storey & Johnson, 1986). Small businesses also tend to be adaptable to changing market conditions and flexible in response to competitive uncertainty (OECD, 1998). In well-established market economies such as the USA, new and small ventures have grown into some of the most successful enterprises listed on the New York Stock Exchange (Schram, 2004).

Given the identified importance of small businesses in both developing and developed economies, it is perhaps not surprising that they have become a focus for government policy in China (*Asia Monitor,* 2003; Economist Intelligence Unit, 2002; Xinhua, 2004). This has been due in part to a desire to identify and encourage new sources of employment, reflecting government concerns that the restructuring of the state-owned sector has led to growing social unrest (Fan, 2003). The laying-off of workers from state-owned enterprises has increased unemployment, mainly in urban areas (*China Statistical Yearbook*, 2001: 107). There is also extensive rural unemployment, which has led to the migration of rural workers to more prosperous areas (Guang, 2001). Concerns about lower economic growth inland and away from the eastern seaboard have led to preferential policies that encourage investment and economic development in China's western provinces (Goodman, 2004; Tan, 2004).

Policy interest in enterprise development can be seen in the passing and promulgation of the SME Promotion Law,[3] which came into effect in January 2003. This law provides a framework for government recognition and support of small and medium enterprises. The law identifies small and medium enterprises as an important component of the national economy, particularly because of their role in *'expanding job opportunities in both urban and rural areas'*. The SME Promotion Law highlights the importance of active support to small businesses via the development of effective business support services (Chapters III & VI) and the development of a market for these services (Chapter V).

This law provides a framework for government recognition and support of small and medium enterprises and recognizes a role for government in supporting private sector development. It establishes several underpinning principles: that government will play a proactive and constructive role in encouraging and enabling small and medium enterprise development (Article 22); that multiple measures and approaches will be adopted; some of which involve direct engagement with enterprises (Articles 38–42); that some of these measures will involve government stimulation of a 'market' for private sector consumption of services to businesses (Article 39), as well as development of the broader business climate and environment through policy promulgation (e.g. Article 29), and fiscal measures (Article 23). Embedded within the SME Promotion Law is a commitment to developing systems to support small and medium-sized enterprises at local government level throughout China.

*Theoretical Propositions: Conditions Affecting Institutional Emergence*

Chinese government at local level has traditionally been heavily involved in local economic development, via control over the management of the enterprise sector (e.g. Oi, 1995; Unger & Chan, 1999). As restructuring of the state-owned sector has unfolded, leading to changes in ownership structure and the 'release' of smaller enterprises, direct control by local government over corporate decision-making has reduced. The influence of government, however, continues to be strong, albeit in more indirect ways, including: control over local regulation and compliance requirements; local tax-raising powers; the opportunities for access to resources and clients through close ties with government; the benefits of public recognition by government of the importance and value of enterprise development to local economic development. For the enterprise development centres that are the focus of this paper, the relationship with government was therefore seen as important for initial emergence and survival. There is however a perceived 'trade-off' between the importance of good relations with government and an ability to maintain operational autonomy. Two key propositions are explored in this article in connection with relationships with local government:

*Proposition 1.* Good relationships with government are important for new institutions during their emergence in China, because this provides access to resources, and clients, as well as local recognition within government.

*Proposition 2.* With the advent of the SME Promotion Law, which identifies government as the co-ordinator of local SME support systems, there is a possibility that close relationships with government will lead to reduced autonomy, and hence a limit to an organization's ability to operate flexibly in response to client needs, indicating a 'trade-off' between autonomy and good relations.

Local economic conditions vary significantly within China, with the majority of growth and liberalization occurring along the coast and in local concentrations of entrepreneurial activity. Provision of professional business services, such as consultancy and advisory services, has tended to be concentrated in areas of rapid economic growth. In local economies where growth has been slower, and the number and importance of private businesses is relatively low, such services are unlikely to be available:

*Proposition 3*: Where local economic conditions are conducive to the growth of the private sector, and the emergence of advisory and related business services, enterprise development centres are more likely to experience positive demand and responses from clients.

## Data Collection and Analysis

Data were collected through a series of face-to-face interviews with staff from the six enterprise development centres, and with partners and stakeholders, in particular those in local government. For each centre, two rounds of interviews were undertaken, each over a full working day. The most common schedule involved an initial interview with the director of the centre, followed by a meeting with staff, and then consultations with local government counterparts and partners. A final interview was then held with each centre director, in many cases with one or more members of staff present.

The typical structure for each interview was to start by inviting each interviewee to comment on and describe their respective centre. The interviewers then followed up by seeking clarification on particular points, as raised. To conclude the interview, participants were asked to evaluate the current performance of the centres and to provide examples and evidence to support their responses. The result was a series of detailed notes for each interview which were then compared and cross-referenced by the authors. The first round of interviews was followed by a second round between four and six months later.

The data collected were extensive, in that they are based on transcripts of two full days of interviews for each centre. The authors also followed up with emails and telephone contact, in order to clarify areas of potential ambiguity and gaps in the information collected. In total, over 60 hours of interviews were undertaken across all six centres.

### Establishing Enterprise Centres in Liaoning and Sichuan

The six centres predated the SME Promotion Law of 2003, and were established within the context of rapid restructuring of the state-owned sector in the second half of the 1990s. Their creation was related explicitly to the need to create more favourable local conditions for business start-up and growth as well as alternative sources of employment, to off-set the laying off of workers by state-owned enterprises. The centres were established in six cities in two provinces of China (Liaoning and Sichuan) between August 2000 and November 2000.

Initially named Information and Advice Centres, the Liaoning province institutions renamed themselves Business Advice Centres.[4] In Sichuan Province, the three centres called themselves Enterprise Development and Advice Centres.[5] These name changes distinguished the institutions from the municipal Information and Advice Centres that were established by local government to provide information – typically around regulations and government procedures – to enterprises. The amended names reflected an explicit focus on business and enterprise development, rather than on the provision and circulation of information to smaller enterprises.

By their fourth year of operation, all centres had developed a portfolio of enterprise development services (see Tables 1 and 2). The client groups for the centres tended to be medium-sized and small and micro enterprises, predominantly but not exclusively privately-owned. Contracts ranged from 10,000 Renminbi up to 300,000 to 400,000 Renminbi, with the majority between 10,000 and 100,000 Renminbi. Medium-sized enterprises, which were categorized by the Centres as having up to 500 employees, were the main source of larger contracts. Many large contracts were not as profitable as expected, however, as they entailed extensive input by centre staff, and clients tended to be especially demanding.

Commercially viable services focused on business improvement consultancy as well as on areas of functional specialization where clients had identified specific needs and, typically, lacked the required knowledge and experience within their own enterprises. Business improvement contracts tended to focus on increasing the profitability and overall competitiveness of client businesses. More specialist consultancy and advice focused on three areas: marketing; financial management; and human resource management. In broad terms, businesses were interested in marketing consultancy and advice because they tended to lack skills and knowledge in new market development, and because competition in local markets was intensifying as a result of the growing number of new entrants, both indigenous and external. Client interest in financial management advice and consultancy tended to arise out of a desire to establish effective finance systems in businesses, and reflected the lack of development of the actuarial profession in China. Businesses used the centres' consultancy and advice services in human resource development to develop clearer job descriptions and rewards and incentive schemes for their own staff.

*Key Factors Determining Advice Centre Emergence*

The patterns of emergence and performance of the centres in their first four years of operation varied considerably. Chengdu, for example, rapidly became commercially sustainable and developed a strong market profile. Others experienced periods of difficulty and crisis in emergence, for multiple reasons. Based on management data produced by the centres, as well as interviews with centre staff and stakeholders, a series of factors were identified that determined the development of the institutions (see Table 3 for an assessment of each centre against these factors)

**Table 1.** Services offered by Liaoning Business Advice Centres by Year 4 (2003)

| | Anshan | Dalian | Shenyang |
|---|---|---|---|
| Service | *Business Performance Improvement Consultancy* | *Business Performance Improvement Consultancy* | *Business Performance Improvement Consultancy* |
| Client | Medium and larger small enterprises, all sectors mostly manufacturing, Anshan and Haicheng Municipalities | Medium and larger small enterprises, all sectors mostly manufacturing, Dalian city | Medium and larger small enterprises, all sectors. Some government department and state–owned enterprises as clients |
| Fees | RMB 30,000–350,000 | RMB 30,000–350,000 | RMB 10,000–300,000. Government services supported by subsidy. |
| Service | *Marketing Consultancy/Advice* | *Marketing Consultancy/Advice* | *Marketing Consultancy/Advice* |
| Client | Medium and larger small enterprises, all sectors, mostly manufacturing, Anshan Municipality | Medium and larger small enterprises, all sectors | Medium and small enterprises, all sectors |
| Fees | RMB 10,000–300,000 | RMB 10,000–200,000 | RMB 10,000–300,000 |
| Service | *Financial Management Consultancy/Advice* | *Financial Management Consultancy/ Advice* | *Financial Management Consultancy/Advice* |
| Client | Medium and larger small enterprises, all sectors mostly manufacturing | Medium and small enterprises, all sectors | Medium and larger small enterprises, all sectors, but predominantly services |
| Fees | RMB 10,000–300,000 | RMB 10,000–200,000 | RMB 10,000–300,000 |
| Service | *Human Resources Management Consultancy/Advice* | *Human Resources Management Consultancy/Advice* | *Human Resources Management Consultancy/Advice* |
| Client | Medium and larger small enterprises, all sectors mostly manufacturing | Medium and small enterprises, all sectors mostly manufacturing | Medium and larger small enterprises, all sectors. |
| Fees | RMB 10,000–300,000 | RMB 10,000–200,000 | RMB 10,000–300,000 |

| | | | |
|---|---|---|---|
| Service | *Start-up Training* | *Start-up Training* | *Start-up Training* |
| Client | Potential start-ups, mainly laid off workers | Potential start-ups, mainly graduates as well as high-tech and IT target sectors. | Potential start-ups, including laid off workers |
| Fees | Free delivery, supported by payment from local government. | Free delivery, supported by small government in kind subsidy | Free delivery, supported by local government subsidy |
| Service | *Specialized Training* | *Tailored training* | *Tailored Training* |
| Client | Specific sectors, e.g. hotel and restaurant – micro and small enterprises | Small and medium enterprises | Medium and larger Small Enterprises – all sectors. Some Government Department and SOE clients |
| Fees | Based on cost recovery, dependent on size of groups | RMB 10,000–50,000 | RMB 10,000–50,000 |
| Service | *Counselling membership service* | | |
| Client | Micro and Small Enterprises | | |
| Fees | Up to RMB 12,000 per enterprise per year | | |

**Table 2.** Services offered by Sichuan Enterprise Development and Advice Centre Services by Year 4 (2003)

|  | Chengdu | Leshan | Mianyang |
|---|---|---|---|
| Service | *Business Performance Improvement Consultancy* | *General Business Advice and Consultancy* | *Business Performance Improvement Consultancy* |
| Client | Medium enterprises, all sectors, Chengdu municipality | Small enterprises, mostly private and TVEs | Medium and larger small enterprises, all sectors |
| Fees | RMB 50,000–400,000 | RMB10,000–100,000 | RMB 30,000–400,000 |
| Service | *Marketing Consultancy/Advice* | *Marketing Consultancy/Advice* | *Marketing Consultancy/Advice* |
| Client | Medium and larger small enterprises, all sectors but predominantly services and IT | Small enterprises, mostly private and TVEs | Medium and larger small enterprises, all sectors, but predominantly services |
| Fees | RMB 10,000–300,000 | RMB10,000–100,000 | RMB 10,000–300,000 |
| Service | *Financial Management Consultancy/Advice* | *Financial Management Consultancy/Advice* | *Financial Management Consultancy/Advice* |
| Client | Medium and larger Small Enterprises – all sectors but predominantly service and IT | Small Enterprises, mostly private and TVEs | Medium and Larger Small Enterprises – all sectors, but predominantly services |
| Fees | RMB 10–300,000 | RMB 10,000–100,000 | RMB 10,000–300,000 |
| Service | *Human Resources Management Consultancy/Advice* | *Human Resources Management Consultancy/ Advice* | *Human Resources Management Consultancy/Advice* |
| Client | Medium and larger small enterprises, all sectors but predominantly services and IT | Small enterprises, mostly private and TVEs | Medium and larger small enterprises, all sectors but predominantly services |
| Fees | RMB 10,000–300,000 | RMB 10,000–100,000 | RMB 10,000–300,000 |

| | | | |
|---|---|---|---|
| Service | *Start-up Training* | *Start-up Training* | *Start-up Training* |
| Client | New ventures and potential start ups | Potential start-ups, mainly laid off workers and peasants | Potential start-ups, including laid off workers |
| Fees | Free delivery. 1 paid course for army dependents. Most courses non-fee earning. | Free delivery, supported by annual payment of up to RMB 150,000 by local government. Some courses non-fee earning. | Free delivery, supported by annual payment of up to RMB 100,000 by local government. |
| Service | *Sales and Marketing, Finance Training Course* | | |
| Client | Medium and larger small enterprises, all sectors but predominantly services and IT | | |
| Fees | RMB 10,000–50,000 | | |
| Service | *Tailored Training* | *Tailored Training* | *Tailored Training* |
| Client | Small enterprises, mostly private and TVEs | Small enterprises, mostly private and TVEs | Small enterprises, usually members of trade associations with links to Enterprise Centre |
| Fees | RMB10,000–50,000 | RMB10,000–50,000 | RMB10,000–50,000, paid by members |

**Table 3.** Assessment of Advice Centres by Component

| | Chengdu | Leshan | Mianyang | Anshan | Dalian | Shenyang |
|---|---|---|---|---|---|---|
| *Leadership* | Entrepreneurial leader following replacement of first director | 3 directors; last in place since 09/02 uses *guanxi* for business development | 1 director: shift from authoritarian approach to facilitator | 1 director: shift from hierarchical approach to 'professional' development of team | Conflict over AC direction resolved by recruitment of new director | 2 directors, largely under influence of municipal government |
| *Team* | Competent & motivated. Staff turnover in later years of operation | High turnover of non-local (Chengdu) staff early on. Small team – local recruitment difficult | High turnover for first 3 years. Stable team of local staff now – local recruitment difficult | Stable team throughout – with additional staff from another institution joining in year 4 | High turnover first 2 years – followed by smaller more stable team | Some staff turnover – new staff lacked SME development knowledge and experience |
| *Business model* | Own delivery, fully commercial – moving to larger contracts (>100,000 RMB) | Medium commercial contracts (circa 40k) with strong government contacts (10% income) | Own delivery on smaller contracts to reflect capacity (initially pursued large contracts) | Own delivery – mostly commercial work from SMEs. Some contract training from government | Moved from own delivery to more sub-contracting | Own delivery. Received donor funding to undertake commissioned contracts for local government |
| *Relationships* | Initially difficult relationship with government now largely neutral | Problematic relationship for first 2 years resolved by appointment of new director with government links | Strong relationship through legal representative | Gradual strength-ening of relation-ship with municipal government | Challenging at start, due to split between AC board and MPMO | Strong relationship with local government, which has control over AC & is increasingly supportive |

| | | | | | | |
|---|---|---|---|---|---|---|
| *'Offer'* | Mainly consultancy & advice for SMEs. Some training and fewer 'open' workshops | Advice and consultancy. Start-up training programmes | Advice and consultancy | Advice and consultancy. Some training. Start-up programmes | Advice and consultancy | Advice and consultancy |
| *Market makers* | Open workshops for business development & business health checks | Shifted from direct approaches to businesses to open workshops and referral from government | Initially based on referrals and existing networks. Changed to proactive use of health checks and open workshops | Little market development initially, but then used open workshops & seminars | Workshops & company visits | Some health checks and workshops. Reliance on municipal government |

*Effective leadership.* In several centres, directors were replaced or removed as a result of breakdown in relationships with staff. In institutions that experienced high turnover of directors, such as Dalian and Leshan, initial progress in developing the organization and its activities was limited. Successful institutional development required continuity in leadership. Although approaches to and styles of leadership varied, effective directors had a vision for the centre and its development, as well as good relations with staff.

*Capable and motivated/committed team.* Retention of staff, and the development of their capability and knowledge of enterprise development, were important aspects of institutional emergence. Most centres experienced periods of turnover and loss of staff, typically for three reasons:

1.  perceptions that leadership was poor or weak;
2.  disagreements with the director and key staff;
3.  mis-match between personal expectations of job and role requirements as dictated by the centres.

Effective teams tended to work in small groups on joint projects, and developed a shared understanding of enterprise development via shared experiential learning.

*Viable 'business model'*, including a strategy for achieving financial sustainability. Of particular concern to the staff of the centres early in the project was the institution's prospects for survival. There was a preoccupation with income generation in order to cover costs. Most centres sought a 'mixed' funding model, with income from business clients combined with contracts from local government and other 'third party' sources (i.e. commissioned work). Many of the centres sought to cross-subsidize less commercially viable work, such as business start-up training, with consulting contracts for medium enterprises and larger small businesses.

*Effective relationships* with local stakeholders, especially government. For those centres that associated themselves closely with government (see Figure 1), relationships with key contacts were of particular importance. Although these relations did not lead to the provision of funding for most of the centres, they provided multiple forms of *guanxi*, i.e. relationally-driven favours, such as referral of businesses to the institutions by government officials, and support for activities and events (Yang, 2002).

*Appropriate and viable 'offer'*, i.e. products and services. The planned portfolio of services and activities was modified, in some cases extensively, by staff in the centres as they became more familiar with businesses. To some extent, these changes reflected articulated need, as indicated by businesses with which centre staff interacted. Changes to the 'offer' also reflected existing expertise within the centre, with some centres developing services based on the specialist knowledge and experience of staff.

*Proactive market development* and *'market-making'*. Staff in the centres found that most prospective clients had no or little previous experience of purchasing and using business development services such as consultancy and training. A lack of awareness among smaller businesses of specific providers of business

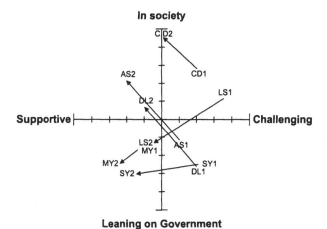

**Figure 1.** Relationships between government and centres *Glossary*: AS = Anshan (Liaoning Province); Chengdu (Sichuan Province); DL = Dalian (Liaoning); LS = Leshan (Sichuan); MY = Mianyang (Sichuan); SY = Shenyang (Liaoning).

development services is typical in many countries. However, the lack of other institutions and the novelty of the concept of enterprise development in China during the early stages of institutional development meant that there was no tradition and little precedent among firms of purchasing advisory and support services. In many cases, staff had to explain and convince prospective clients of the benefits and nature of business development services as a novel concept or notion, as well as the specific services offered.

## Effects of Relationships with Municipal Government on Institutional Emergence

Interactions with local government strongly influenced the centres, particularly in their early years of establishment. Each municipal government registered the centres and took responsibility for their legal status, and so played a governance role that provided them with a degree of control over the institutions. The nature of this relationship varied considerably, from centres that were operating 'in society', i.e. outside the parameters of government with minimal intervention, to those that were 'leaning on government', i.e. closely associated with and influenced by government. Centres that leant on government tended to be located in government buildings, and in some cases, became subsumed into wider networks of government and quasi-government institutions. An organ of local government became the major 'shareholder' in the centre, appointing its representatives as legal representatives in the case of 'third sector' (*shiye*) institutions in Sichuan, and as chair of the board in registered companies in Liaoning.

The overall disposition of local government counterparts towards the centre was a significant factor in their emergence and development. In some cases, relationships with local government were positive, in that officials were supportive of the centres and their objectives. In other cases, the relationship was less supportive, typically for two reasons:

1.  desire to control the centre and place it within the structure of municipal government;
2.  lack of understanding of the rationale for the centres and their objectives and *modus operandi*.

The six centres were mapped against both of these dimensions of their relationship with government (see Figure 1). Each centre was plotted twice, in order to map and hence illustrate changes in their relationship with government from the first to fourth year of operation. Apart from Mianyang, all the Advice Centres started with a relationship that was more challenging than supportive. For example, attempts were made to control expenditure and receipt of income and funds through local government accounting procedures. As the centres developed, and as understanding of and support for their role in local economic development grew, the relationship with government improved. Parts of municipal government that interacted regularly with staff became more familiar with, and thus sympathetic towards, the centres. As the centres established themselves, and as enterprise development became a policy focus that local government was mandated through legislation to act on, recognition of and support for the centres increased.

One example of this was the engagement of several of the centres to deliver start-up training on behalf of the local Labour Bureau. At national level, the Ministry of Labour and Social Security had developed a view that business start-up and self-employment, particularly for laid-off workers, could address the increase in unemployment that followed on from state-owned enterprise restructuring (Fan, 2003). One outcome was the delivery of business start-up training locally through municipal Labour Bureaux. Via referrals within government, two of the centres were asked to deliver this training, in large part because the centres were seen as entities that specialized in enterprise development, including support for start-ups.

Of the six centres, two started operation more 'in society' than 'leaning on government'. Chengdu and Leshan, both in Sichuan Province, were established as distinctive and autonomous institutions that were expected to support themselves outside of government structures. In Chengdu, relationships between the centre and local government representatives broke down at an early stage. Indeed, by year four, there was no interaction between Chengdu Enterprise Development and Advice Centre and the municipal government, and the centre was exploring options for changing the ownership structure to that of a private venture, via employee purchase of shares. In Leshan, municipal government responsibility for the centre moved from the local bureau of the State Economic and Trade Commission to the Leshan Commission of Foreign Trade and Economic Cooperation, in order to enable the centre to operate more independently.

The other four institutions initially 'leant on government', i.e. they had a close and dependent relationship with municipal government. Over their first four years, however, the nature of these relationships changed, in some cases considerably. Anshan and Dalian became more independent and relationships with government improved. By year four, these centres were operating autonomously, and had supportive government relations. The second broad trend, which involved Leshan, Mianyang and Shenyang, was to increased reliance on government, in particular via established governance relationships. These three institutions saw improvements in their relationships with government, primarily for two reasons:

1. a growing commitment to the centres, as they demonstrated their ability to survive and, equally important, to become sustainable (rather than being dependent on funding and other support from local government);
2. growing acceptance of and interest in private sector development in government, due in part to the SME Promotion Law as well as initiatives from central government bodies, such as the start-up work of the Ministry of Labour and Social Security.

## *Influence of Local Economic Conditions on Institutional Emergence*

The centres that leaned more on government over the period appear to have done so as a survival strategy. All three of the institutions that reinforced their relationship with government (Leshan, Mianyang and Shenyang) operated in difficult market conditions for their first few years (see Figure 2). In part, these conditions were due to depression in the local economy: in Mianyang and Shenyang because of under-performance in and restructuring of the state enterprise sector; and in Leshan because it is a relatively isolated and rural city that had not benefited from the growth effects of Chengdu and Chongqing, the closest major urban areas. Of the three that moved more 'into society', only Anshan faced a depressed and hence difficult local economy (due to the restructuring of the city's state-owned enterprises, in particular Anshan Iron and Steel). The other two centres, namely Chengdu and Dalian, operated in city economies that have been growing rapidly in recent years.

Market conditions improved in all six municipalities between 2000 and 2003 (as can be seen in Figure 2). The rate of improvement varied between municipalities, however, and in two cities (Anshan and Mianyang) continued to be difficult throughout the period. Conditions in two other cities – Chengdu and

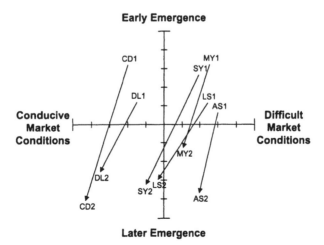

**Figure 2.** Effects of local market conditions on early and later emergence

Dalian – became increasingly conducive, although the Chengdu Enterprise Development and Advice Centre out-performed the Dalian Advice Centre. Three centres (Anshan, Leshan and Dalian) markedly improved their later performance, even though market conditions in Anshan and Leshan were poor or not conducive to institutional development. The marked improvement for these two centres indicates that performance related not just to external dynamics, but also to the development of the institution itself and to establishing a profile and reputation among business clients. Although Shenyang appears relatively stable, with positive early and later emergence, the centre under-performed between these two points, i.e. in years two and three, and faced difficulties in generating income and retaining staff. The situation improved towards the end of the period as an effective director was appointed, staff turnover fell and relationships with government became more supportive.

### Testing the Propositions: Implications for Enterprise Development Institutions in China

Overall, the early patterns of emergence of the Advice Centres support Proposition 1, in that recognition by and support from local government assisted in their initial development. For most Centres – in particular Anshan, Mianyang, and Shenyang – strong ties with municipal government provided access to resources, such as donor funding (Shenyang) and training contracts (Anshan), as well as introductions to clients (Mianyang). The exception was Chengdu Enterprise Development and Advice Centre, which broke all ties with the municipal government, in large part because municipal government counterparts were not supportive of the idea of small business development and preferred to focus on the state-owned sector.

Proposition 2 postulated that local government may seek to control the institutions within the frame of the SME Promotion Law. For some institutions, such as Dalian and Leshan, overly close relations with local government led to interference in the operations of the centres. In other institutions, in particular Mianyang and Shenyang, close ties with government brought real and substantive advantages, including funding and informal support, that enabled survival of the centres. The distinguishing criterion affecting relations with government appeared to be the extent to which local counterparts understood and sympathized with the objectives and rationale of the advice centres. Where close ties with government were generally positive, officials supported the concepts underpinning the centres, and saw them as contributing to local economic development.

As suggested in Proposition 3, local market conditions, i.e. the extent to which there was a growing private sector that was able and willing to pay for business development services, were a major factor in influencing the development of the centres. Where local growth of the private, small business population was strong, and led to the emergence of private advisers, consultants and professional service providers, overall demand for enterprise development services grew more rapidly than in municipalities where the private sector was not as well represented.

**Implications: Experiential Learning and Capacity-Building in the Centres**

The centres were originally established in 2000, at a time when there was little familiarity with the concepts of enterprise development and the provision of business development services to smaller enterprises in China. Similar organizations, such as incubators and workspaces established as part of the 'Torch' programme to encourage more high-technology start-ups, were in their early stages of development (Harwitt, 2002). At that time, support for small businesses was limited to income tax exemptions or reductions, and new forms of private and quasi-private ownership, such as joint stock companies (Fan, 2003; Lau *et al.*, 1999).

Reflecting the lack of an established network of similar agencies across China, staff recruited into the institutions tended not to have previous experience of enterprise development and the provision of business development services. Most were appointed on the basis of transferable skills developed while working for joint ventures between Chinese and international companies or based on work experience in Chinese consultancy firms. In addition, municipal government stakeholders lacked a policy framework for enterprise development and only had as precedent and example the Information and Advice Centres that were created in order to provide information on planning, regulation and other state procedures.

As the directors of the institutions, and key staff, took responsibility for the development of the centres, they started to develop their own views on and conceptualizations of what the centres should do and how they should operate. Interactions with businesses, as prospective clients as well as fee-paying customers, provided feedback on the nature of demand for services, in many cases leading to changes in emphasis and offer. Most of the centres, for example, developed consultancy services that they offered to medium-sized enterprises (typically with 200 to 500 employees), primarily because these businesses had the resources to pay for services and were able to specify their requirements to staff from the centres.

Formulation of a model and rationale for the centres enabled staff to present services and capabilities in a coherent and clear way, which in turn demonstrated credibility to businesses (see Figure 3). For some institutions, the concept underpinning the centre has remained predominantly with the director or key staff. When the concept was shared, and all staff learned from and through collective and shared experiences, the scope for systematic approaches to new market development expanded. Integral to institutional capacity-building was collective learning that produced a clear and shared concept for the centres that, in turn, enabled experiential learning with and through clients.

**Conclusion: China's New Institutional Framework for Private Sector Development**

The enterprise development centres in Liaoning and Sichuan are examples of an emergent form of institution in China that reflect the changing nature of the economy and its organization, particularly in terms of the role that government plays in economic development. With the withdrawal of state management of

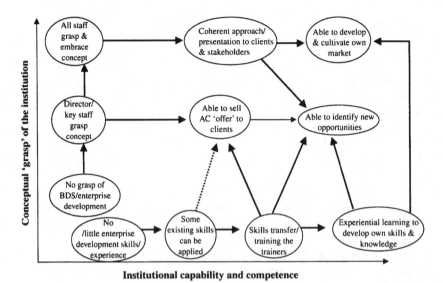

**Figure 3.** Phases of concept and competence development in the advice centres

enterprises, via transfers of ownership of township and village enterprises and smaller formerly state-owned enterprises, the Chinese economy is becoming increasingly dominated by the private sector. The shift in focus by government towards developing a small number of 'national champions' owned by the state (Nolan, 2004) indicates that the rest of the economy will become more removed from public ownership, and hence from direct government control. This suggests a very different relationship between state and markets than existed before 1978 when almost all businesses were publicly-owned, and national economic activity was essentially part of the state.

Within such a scenario, the prospects and paths of development and growth of the private sector become more important as it accounts for an increased share of national output. At the same time, the government's relationship with businesses, and the ways in which it encourages and supports their development are liable to change. In mixed economies, where the private sector accounts for most economic activity and output, governments tend to establish and support 'intermediary' institutions that can work with and enable the development and growth of the private sector. Business development and support institutions are seen, as a result, as integral to economic development in developed economies and fast-developing countries (OECD, 1998; World Bank, 2002).

The centres are models of, and experiments in, establishing intermediary institutions whose remit is to support and stimulate the development of the private sector, in this case in a country where rapid and sustained economic growth has historically suppressed the need for such institutions. The establishment of these new institutions has occurred as the private sector has grown and government has started to withdraw from direct ownership and management of most enterprises. This suggests that the enterprise development centres will become a conduit for the allocation and provision of government, and perhaps social, resources to stimulate economic development through private sector growth and expansion. It points to the possibility that these institutions will become increasingly important to the future economic development of China should overall rates of growth slow and government seek out strategies for stimulating new forms of economic expansion – a characteristic of industrial policy in mature economies such as the UK and the European Union (Department of Trade and Industry, 2003; European Commission, 2003; Organization for Economic Co-operation and Development, 1998).

## Acknowledgements

The authors of this paper were involved in the State-Owned Enterprise Restructuring and Enterprise Development (SOERED) project, a four-year programme of technical assistance funded by the UK Department for International Development (DFID). The findings presented in this paper reflect the views of the authors alone, however, and do not relate to DFID views or policies.

## Notes

[1] The official Chinese definition of small and medium enterprises is as follows: small enterprises have a turnover of up to 30 Renminbi (RMB), medium enterprises from RMB 30 to 300 million (see APEC Centre for Technology Exchange and Training for Small Businesses – http://www.actetsme.org/chin/PRC98.htm for definitions by industrial sector). For the purpose of this article, *getihu* (self-employed or micro-enterprises with fewer than 8 employees) are also included. This is in comparison with OECD and European Commission definitions, which define SMEs as having up to 249 employees (European Commission, 2003; Organization for Economic Co-operation and Development, 1998). Definitions of size of enterprise in China tend to be larger than those adopted in OECD countries. Medium to small SOEs (MSSOEs), for example, tend to be significantly larger than the small and medium enterprise (SME) category used in most mature economies.

[2] Anshan, Dalian and Shenyang municipalities in Liaoning Province, and Chengdu, Leshan and Mianyang in Sichuan Province.

[3] Law of the People's Republic of China on Promoting Small and Medium-sized Enterprises, adopted at the 28th National People's Congress, June 2002, for implementation on Jan. 1, 2003.

[4] The Liaoning centres had slightly different Chinese names, as follows: Anshan Small and Medium Enterprise Development Advisory Consultant Company Limited (*Anshanshi zhongxiao qiye fazhan zixun guwen youxian gongsi*); Dalian Enterprise Development Consultancy Limited Company (*Dalian qiye fazhan zixun youxian gongsi*); Shenyang Modern Business Advisory Company Limited (*Shenyang xiandai qiye zixun youxian gongsi*).

[5] The Sichuan centres had the following Chinese names: Chengdu Edac Enterprise Development Management and Advice Company Limited (*Yida qiye fazhan guanli zixun youxian gongsi*); Leshan Enterprise Development Advice Centre (*Leshan qiye fazhan zixun zhongxin*); Mianyang Enterprise Development Advice Centre (*Mianyang qiye fazhan zixun zhongxin*).

## References

APEC Centre for Technology Exchange and Training for Small and Medium Enterprises. SME profile: People's Republic of China (available at http://www.actetsme.org/chin/PRC98.htm).

Ash, R. (1988) The evolution of agricultural policy, *China Quarterly*, 116, pp. 529–555.

Asia Monitor (2003) China: boost to private sector, *Asia Monitor: China and North East Asia Monitor*, 10(1), pp. 1–3.

Bear, M., Gibson, A. & Hitchins, R. (2004) From principles to practice: ten critical challenges for BDS market development, *Small Enterprise Development*, 14(4), pp. 10–23.

Birch, D. (1979) *The Job Creation Process* (Cambridge, MA: MIT Press).

Broesma, L. & Gautier, P. (1997) Job creation and job destruction by small firms: an empirical investigation for the Dutch manufacturing sector, *Small Business Economics*, 9(3), pp. 211–224.

Cheng, Y. & Lo, D. (2002) Explaining the financial performance of China's industrial enterprises: beyond the competition–ownership controversy, *China Quarterly*, 170, pp. 413–440.

*China Statistical Yearbook* (2001) (Beijing: China Statistical Publishing House).

Cooke, F. (2005) Employment relations in small commercial businesses in China, *Industrial Relations Journal*, 36(1), pp. 19–37.

Department of Trade and Industry (D.T.I.) (2003) *A Government Action Plan for Small Business* (London: The Stationery Office).

Department of Trade and Industry (D.T.I.) (2001) *Opportunity for All in a World of Change* (London: The Stationery Office).

Dickson, B. (2003) *Red Capitalists in China* (Cambridge: Cambridge University Press).

*Economist, The* (2004a) The great leap forward, *The Economist*, 30 Sept.

*Economist, The* (2004b) On the capitalist road, *The Economist*, 18 March.

*Economist, The* (2000) Private salvation?, *The Economist*, 6 April.

Economist Intelligence Unit (2002) China: a boost for the private sector?, *Country Monitor*, 18, Nov.

European Commission (E.C.) (2003) *Green Paper on Entrepreneurship* (Brussels: COM (2003) 27 Final).

Fan, C. (2003) Government support for small and medium-sized enterprises in China, *Problems of Economic Transition*, 45(11), pp. 51–58.

Gallagher, C., Daly, M. & Thompson, J. (1991) The growth of UK companies and their contribution to job creation, *Small Business Economics*, 3(4), pp. 269–286.

Garnaut, R., Song, L., Yao, Y. & Wang, X. (2001) *Private Enterprise in China* (Canberra: Asia Pacific Press, and Beijing: Peking University Centre for Social Research).

Gibb, A. & Li, J. (2003) Organizing for enterprise in China: what can we learn from the Chinese micro, small and medium enterprise development experience, *Futures*, 35(4), pp. 403–421.

Gold, T. (1991) Urban private business and social change, in: D. Davis & E. Vogel (Eds) *Chinese Society on the Eve of Tiananmen: The Impact of Reform* (Harvard, MA: Council on East Asian Studies, Harvard University).

Goodman, D. (2004) The campaign to 'Open Up the West': national, provincial-level and local perspectives, *China Quarterly*, 178 (June), pp. 317–334.

Gregory, N. & Tenev, S. (2001) China's home-grown entrepreneurs, *China Business Review*, Jan–Feb, pp. 14–18.

Guang, L. (2001) Reconstituting the rural urban divide: peasant migration and the rise of orderly migration in contemporary China, *Journal of Contemporary China*, 10(28), pp. 471–493.

Harwitt, E. (2002) High-technology incubators: fuel for China's new entrepreneurship?, *China Business Review*, July–Aug, pp. 26–29.

Heshmati, A. (2001) On the growth of micro and small firms: evidence from Sweden, *Small Business Economics*, 17(3), pp. 213–228.

Hohti, S. (2000) Job flows and job quality by establishment size in the Finnish manufacturing sector, *Small Business Economics*, 15(4), pp. 265–294.

Hughes, N. (2002) *China's Economic Challenge: Smashing the Iron Rice Bowl* (New York: East Gate Books).

Konings, J. (1995) Gross job flows and the evolution of size in UK establishments, *Small Business Economics*, 7(3), pp. 213–220.

Kwong, C. & Lee, P. (2000) Business–government relations in industrializing rural China: a principal–agent perspective, *Journal of Contemporary China*, 9(25), pp. 513–534.

Lau, C., Ngo, H. & Chow, C. (1999) Private Businesses in China: Emergent Environment and Managerial Behaviour, in: L. Kelly & Y. Luo (Eds) *China 2000: Emerging Business Issues* (Thousand Oaks, CA: Sage Publications).

Li, H. & Rozelle, S. (2003) Privatizing rural China: insider privatization, innovative contracts and the performance of township enterprises, *The China Quarterly*, 176(Dec), pp. 981–1005.

Lin, W. & Chen, T. (2004) China's widening economic disparities and its go west program, *Journal of Contemporary China*, 13(41), pp. 663–686.

Liu, Y. (1992) Reform from below: the private economy and local politics in the rural industrialization of Wenzhou, *China Quarterly*, 130 (June), pp. 293–316.

Ministry of Economic Trade and Industry (2002) *White Paper on Small and Medium Enterprises in Japan*, available at www.meti.go.jp/english/report/

Nathan, A. & Gilley, B. (2003) *China's New Rulers: The Secret Files* (New York: New York Review of Books).

Nolan, P. (2004) *China at the Crossroads* (Cambridge: Polity Press).

Nolan, P. & Dong, F. (Eds) (1990) *Market Forces in China: Competition and Small Business – The Wenzhou Debate* (London: Zed Books).

Oi, J. (1995) The role of the local state in China's transition economy, *China Quarterly*, 144 (Dec.), pp. 1132–1149.

Organization for Economic Co-operation and Development (OECD) (1998) *Fostering Entrepreneurship* (Paris: OECD).

Parris, K. (1993) Local initiative and national reform: the Wenzhou model of development, *China Quarterly*, 134 (June), pp. 242–263.

Propopenko, J. (2004) *Privatization: Lessons from China and Russia* (Geneva: ILO Enterprise and Management Development Paper (EMD/24/E)).

Schram, S. (2004) Building entrepreneurial economies, *Foreign Affairs*, July/August, pp. 104–115.

Smith, R. & Zhai, Q. (2003) Economic restructuring in China's large and medium-sized state-owned enterprises: evidence from Liaoning, *Journal of Contemporary China*, 12(34), pp. 173–205.

SME Promotion Law, twenty eighth meeting of the standing committee of the Ninth National People's Congress of the People's Republic of China (2002), Law of the Peoples Republic of China on promotion of small and medium sized enterprises (Order of the President, No. 69) available at http://english.gov.cn/laws/2005-10/08/ content_75040.htm.

Storey, D. & Johnson, S. (1986) Job generation in Britain: A review of recent studies, *International Small Business Journal*, 4(4), pp. 29–46.

Sun, L. (2000) Anticipatory ownership reform driven by competition: China's township – village and private enterprises in the 1990s, *Comparative Economic Studies*, XLII(3), pp. 49–75.

Tan, Q. (2004) China develops its West: motivation, strategy and prospect, *Journal of Contemporary China*, 13(4), pp. 611–636.

Tong, C. (2001) Total factor productivity and its spatial disparity across China's township and village enterprises, *Journal of Contemporary China*, 10(26), pp. 155–172.

Tsai, K. (2002) *Back-Alley Banking: Private Entrepreneurs in China* (Ithaca, NY: Cornell University Press).

Tsang, E. (1994) Threats and opportunities faced by private businesses in China, *Journal of Business Venturing*, 9(5), pp. 451–458.

Unger, J. & Chan, A. (1999) Inheritors of the boom: private enterprise and the role of local government in a rural south China township, *China Journal*, 42 (July), pp. 45–76.

Wang, W. (2004) The development of the non-state owned sector and its impact on economic reform, in: P. Propopenko (Ed.) *Privatization: Lessons from China and Russia* (Geneva: ILO Enterprise and Management Development Paper (EMD/24/E)).

Wiemer, C. & Tian, X. (2001) The measurement of small-scale industry for China's GDP accounts, *China Economic Review*, 12(4), pp. 317–322.

World Bank (2002) *Building Institutions for Markets* (New York: Oxford University Press).

World Bank (2001) *Business Development Services for Small Enterprises: Guiding Principles for Donor Intervention*. Available at www.ilo.org/public/english/employment/ent/papers/guide.htm

Xinhua (2004) Serve enterprises: Chinese government retreats from business intervention, *Xinhua News Services*, 03/11/2004.

Yang, M. (2002) The resilience of *Guanxi* and its new deployments: a critique of some new guanxi scholarship, *China Quarterly*, 170, pp. 459–476.

# Business Crisis and Management Fashion: Korean Companies, Restructuring and Consulting Advice

CHRISTOPHER WRIGHT & SEUNG-HO KWON

## Introduction

The diffusion of management knowledge has become an area of increasing interest for business scholars, given the pace of globalization and debates over the convergence of national economic systems (Guillén, 2001; Strange, 1997; Sturdy, 2004). While significant attention has been directed to the role of multinational companies and international joint ventures in the global diffusion of management knowledge (see for example Child & Rodrigues, 1996; Kostova & Roth, 2002), another group of actors characterized as important conduits and bridges for the international flow of business knowledge are management consultancies (Bessant & Rush, 1995; Morris, 2000). Consultants are seen as important diffusion agents due to their adeptness at popularizing management fashions and transforming abstract concepts into commercial products that are sold to a broad management clientele (Clark & Fincham, 2002; Kipping & Engwall, 2002). Moreover, in their role as fashion setters, consultants are argued to affect the types of ideas that are diffused and the preferred models of organizational restructuring (Abrahamson, 1991, 1996; DiMaggio & Powell, 1983; Huczynski, 1993). With the growth of management consultancies into large, globalized service organizations with thousands of staff located in offices around the world, their impact on the international spread of new management knowledge appears significant (O'Shea & Madigan, 1997). Indeed, management consultants have been portrayed as leading examples of the so-called 'cosmocracy', a new global business elite who trade in and promote the model of a seamless, global economy (Micklethwait & Wooldridge, 2003).

However, despite the focus on management consultants as knowledge diffusion agents, little research has been conducted on this topic outside the major economic centres of the United States and Europe. This raises the question of whether the Western depictions of management fashion and fashion setters such as consultancies, apply similarly within non-Western economic settings. While a significant literature has developed regarding the cultural and institutional barriers to management knowledge diffusion (Guirdham, 1999; Hofstede, 1994), little attempt has been made to apply these insights to management consultants.

In this article we explore the role of Western management consultancies in diffusing management 'best practice' within the Korean business community. In particular, we focus on the use made by large Korean companies of Western consultancies in the aftermath of the 1997 economic crisis. While a simplistic interpretation of management fashion theory would suggest a model of passive adoption of Western 'best practice' by Korean companies, more complex contingent models of management knowledge diffusion stress the potential for the adaptation and rejection of new and foreign models which conflict with prevailing institutional and cultural norms. The Korean example is particularly relevant here, given a strong nationalistic culture and traditional rejection of Western consulting advice. The article begins with a consideration of management fashion theory and the application of this model to transnational studies of management knowledge diffusion. We then provide an overview of the history of Korean industrialization, before examining how the 1997 crisis recast perceptions of management consulting advice. In line with the arguments of management fashion theorists, Korean managers became enthusiastic consumers of consulting services and this was linked to their increasing uncertainty and anxiety following the 1997 economic crisis. In the final section of the article, we analyse the post-crisis reaction of Korean business to Western consulting. Far from being passive adopters of Western fashion, we find Korean managers have been both sceptical and selective in their adoption of consulting advice.

## Management Knowledge Diffusion and Management Fashion

Much recent academic attention has focused on the emergence and diffusion of management ideas and knowledge as fashions or fads and on the actors and institutions which act as fashion setters (see for example Abrahamson, 1991; 1996; Gill & Whittle, 1993; Kieser, 1997; Shapiro, 1996). This literature has argued that recent management practices such as corporate excellence, quality management, business process re-engineering, and knowledge management provide examples of this management fashion process, which like other commodities are created and marketed as essential cure-alls, become increasingly popular among consumers, and then fall out of favour as new and alternative fashions emerge. Such bandwagon effects have also been highlighted in literature which stresses increasing organizational isomorphism due to normative and mimetic pressures (DiMaggio & Powell, 1983).

As Abrahamson (1991; 1996) has argued, the concept of management fashion focuses attention on both the supply and demand aspects of the creation and consumption of management knowledge. The supply side of management fashion includes the activities of management fashion setters such as management gurus and consultants, business schools, book publishers and the media, which are seen to compete in the creation, marketing and diffusion of new management knowledge (see also Alvarez, 1998; Micklethwait & Wooldridge, 1996). At the same time, these fashion setters must also seek to interpret new areas of demand among fashion consumers (managers and businesses). A key dynamic on the demand side comprises both socio-psychological and structural-economic drivers for new management knowledge. Importantly, unlike traditional depictions of management innovation in which the adoption of new ideas and techniques is seen as rational and progressive, management fashion theory suggests managers adopt new fashions for both psychological (uncertainty, anxiety) and symbolic reasons (impress peers and shape the impressions of other stakeholders) (Abrahamson, 1996; Sturdy, 1997).

While exponents of management fashion theory have focused on developments in Western economies, far less attention has been directed to the application of these concepts within non-Western cultural settings. This is an important oversight, as historical research on the global diffusion of management ideas and practices has stressed how different institutional and cultural contexts can result in the delay or even rejection of innovations which conflict with prevailing national or cultural norms (Child, 1981; Guillén, 1994; Littler, 1982). Beyond the simple adoption or rejection of new management techniques, the cross-societal diffusion of management practice often involves both intended and unintended departures from the original model, resulting in a process of imitation, adaptation and innovation (Westney, 1987). Hence, in the Japanese case, Western models of production management were absorbed, adapted, changed and then exported back to the West as further innovations in management technique (Tsutsui, 1998). These historical and comparative studies suggest a very different model of management knowledge diffusion from the management fashion stereotype. Rather than a vision of passive adoption, these studies suggest managers interpret new knowledge in a pragmatic, opportunistic and creative manner (Gabriel, 2002).

However, while different economic and cultural contexts are often viewed as constraining influences on the diffusion of new management knowledge, other research suggests there are factors that may reduce or negate such constraints. Firstly, management knowledge can vary in content from a prescriptive technique to a more general theory or idea system. Indeed, a noticeable trend amongst recent management fashions such as business process re-engineering and corporate excellence has been the ambiguity and malleability of these concepts (Benders, *et al.*, 1998; Werr, *et al.*, 1997; Wright & Kitay, 2004). As Clark (2004) notes, this flexibility leaves room for varying interpretations and potentially broadens the applicability of management fashions within different business and social contexts. Such malleability may then provide greater potential for cross-cultural diffusion than more rigidly defined concepts which clash with their adoptive context.

Secondly, the timing of the diffusion process may be critical in the adoption or rejection of new management knowledge (Kieser, 1997). For instance, in periods of economic crisis or social upheaval the possibilities of overcoming institutional or cultural barriers are greater, in that managers are faced with a highly uncertain environment, are anxious to maintain their jobs, and experience significant pressure for dramatic change. As was demonstrated in the case of the former Eastern Bloc economies in the early 1990s, the diffusion of Western management models was facilitated within such a context of dramatic social and economic upheaval. Local managers sought to maintain their positions through the symbolic, and in some cases more substantive, embrace of Western business practice (Kostera, 1995). Indeed, a number of writers have stressed how the foreign or alien nature of specific ideas and practices may in fact make them more appealing to local consumers (Smith & Meiskins, 1995; Sturdy & Gabriel, 2000). This applies particularly where local practice is seen as backward or has been discredited. The recent popularity of benchmarking and global best practice provide examples of the appeal of foreign innovation for local managers.

Taken together, existing literature suggests that the diffusion of management fashions across varying economic, institutional and cultural contexts is a complex process. On the one hand, new management ideas and practices promoted by fashion setters such as consultants may fail to fit their adoptive context and be delayed or rejected by fashion followers (managers), or in the process of diffusion undergo adaptation and change. On the other hand, the limiting effects of divergent contexts may be reduced or negated by the nature of the fashion itself (for example its malleability), the timing of its diffusion, and the potential attraction of what are perceived as superior foreign or alien practices. In the sections that follow, we explore these issues through an analysis of the role of Western management consultancies as fashion setters in Korea. In particular, we focus on the use made by large Korean companies of Western consultancies in the aftermath of the 1997 economic crisis and explore the reasons for both the adoption and rejection of consulting advice. In analysing this case we seek to explore to what extent, issues of timing, the nature of different management techniques, and the foreign nature of the fashion setters, affect the adoption of management knowledge.

## Methodology

In charting the activities of Western consultancies in Korea, our research methodology involved analysis of published literature as well as interviews with consultants and Korean managers. In terms of published data, we undertook an extensive review of the Korean and international business press before, during, and after the economic crisis, focussing in particular on articles which documented the activities of Western consulting companies in Korean industry, as well as publications by Western consulting companies promoting the need to reform Korean business practice.

To supplement the documentary evidence, semi-structured interviews were also conducted with a range of consultants and client managers. This included interviews with four senior consultants (partners and directors) from three of the major Western consultancies operating in Korea, two senior consultants in a local Korean consultancy, and 14 senior managers from three of the largest Korean business groups. These interviews were conducted during July 2004 in Seoul and Ulsan. Our choice of consultant respondents was guided by the senior role of these individuals and their extensive experience working for major Korean companies before and after the 1997 crisis. Similarly, our choice of client respondents focused on senior strategic and operational managers from one company from each of the three largest Korean business groups. All three companies had experience in engaging Western consultancies to provide advice and assist in implementing organizational change. In the interviews, we explored both the supply and demand factors underlying the provision of consulting services in Korea. On the supply side, we enquired about the strategies that Western consultancies used to sell their services, the types of client relationships they had developed, and some examples of consulting projects they had undertaken in Korea. On the demand side, our interviews with managers explored the reasons for using consultants, examples of consulting projects, and their perceptions of the value of consulting interventions.

## Korean Industrialization, the *Chaebol* And Knowledge Diffusion

Prior to the 1997 economic crisis, the Korean economy was seen as a leading example of the East-Asian economic miracle, which had pursued a pattern of economic development markedly different from developed Western economies. As Shin and Chang (2003) highlight, the Korean model of rapid industrialization and economic growth from the 1960s onwards involved a substituting strategy that focused on the rapid development of internationally competitive and export oriented construction and manufacturing industries (shipbuilding, car manufacture) and more recently electronics and semi-conductor manufacture.

Underpinning this model of economic development was a specific configuration of institutions, what has been termed the state-banks-*chaebol* nexus (Shin and Chang, 2003: 13). During the 1960s and 1970s, the Korean state played a central role in shaping the pattern of industrial development through a highly interventionist industry policy. This strategy of industrialization was underwritten by the lending policies of nationalized commercial banks and the *chaebol*, large family-owned and highly diversified conglomerates that were the engines of Korean industrial development. During the 1970s and 1980s, the *chaebol* and the Korean economy grew at a rapid rate, assisted by an authoritarian state and the repression of independent trade unions that ensured a compliant and low-cost workforce (Koo, 2001; Kwon & O'Donnell, 2001). The Korean model of economic development differed from its Asian neighbours in two important respects. First, unlike Singapore and Taiwan, the Korean approach was dominantly nationalistic and independent. While the Korean *chaebol* imported foreign technology, foreign direct investment via multinational companies was constrained by the Korean government. Second, the *chaebol* dominated the Korean economy and small and medium-sized enterprises remained weak and underdeveloped (Shin & Chang, 2003; Whitley, 1999).

The specific nature of Korean economic development shaped the ways in which management knowledge and expertise were diffused. As noted above, the role of foreign capital and multinational companies was limited in the process of Korean industrialization (Kim, 1997: 39–44). While Ernst (2001) highlights how the establishment of electronics manufacture in Korea during the early 1970s, benefited from foreign direct investment by several US semi-conductor firms, in general Western multinationals failed to establish a significant presence within the Korean economy. A major reason for this was the industry policy of the Korean state which concentrated on a fast catch-up strategy in which Korean firms would become low-cost followers for standard, mass-produced products (Ernst, 2001: 141). Rather than relying on the establishment of local subsidiaries by foreign multinationals, the Korean government promoted selected *chaebol* to develop their expertise in new industries through technology licensing arrangements and in some cases, minority joint venture partnerships. In entering new industries and types of production, leading *chaebol* signed licensing agreements with overseas firms, taking advantage of foreign technology and managerial know-how, which they then absorbed and internalized; what Amsden has termed 'learning-by-doing' (Amsden, 1989: 266–7 & 276–80; Kim, 1997). For instance in the case of Hyundai, which began as a construction company, the diversification into car manufacture involved assembly and technological cooperation agreements with a range of American, Japanese and European car producers, and the hiring of overseas engineers for fixed periods (Amsden, 1989: 175–6; Kim, 1997: 110–112; Kwon & O'Donnell, 2001: 58–9).

Added to this, the vertically and horizontally diversified nature of the *chaebol* business groups also encouraged a greater emphasis on internal innovation and knowledge sharing than has traditionally been the case in Western economies; a process of 'institutional innovation' (Shin & Chang, 2003: 27). A prime example was the way in which managers and skilled employees were often transferred within the *chaebol* business group to assist in the development of new industrial ventures. For instance in the case of Hyundai's entry into shipbuilding in the mid-1970s, Amsden (1989: 286–7) notes how skilled staff and managers from a range of Hyundai's other businesses were involved in the construction of the company's new shipyard and provided technical assistance in assembly line and training practices. The size and scale of leading *chaebol*, also enabled the development of significant management development and training programmes that acted as alternatives to the Western business school model of management education (Khanna & Palepu, 1999: 129). While some observers have criticized this pattern of knowledge transfer and industry development as resulting in a narrow knowledge base and sticky specialization focused on low-cost, mass production (Ernst, 2001), others have defended the efficacy of the Korean model as an example of successful late economic development (Shin & Chang, 2003).

Given the distinctive pattern of Korean economic development and the emphasis on the internal development of managerial expertise within the *chaebol*, it is not surprising that prior to the 1990s, Western management consultancies found limited demand for their services and failed to establish a presence in Korea. Several factors were important here. First, the weak role of foreign direct investment severely limited the ability of Western consultancies to gain a foothold in the Korean market. As Kipping (1999) has demonstrated in his historical analysis of the diffusion of American consultancies to Europe, one of the main bridges for the spread of consulting services between countries and continents has been foreign direct investment by multinational companies. Similarly, the spread of British and American consulting services into the Asia–Pacific and African regions also occurred through linkages with multinational companies (Wright, 2002). The lack of such multinational clients in Korea removed one of the key market entry strategies of Western consultancies. Indeed, until the late 1980s, the Korean government prohibited the establishment of local offices by foreign service providers, which meant that when they did work for Korean companies, Western consultancies had to fly in teams of consultants from other Asian offices such as Hong Kong or Tokyo (McKinsey & Company, 2003a).

Second, the extraordinary growth of the Korean *chaebol* from the 1960s to 1980s and their success in rapidly industrializing and competing on global export markets also made them more resistant to external managerial advice (outside specialized technical expertise). Indeed, the very different industrial structure and patterns of business ownership within the Korean economy appear to have limited the applicability of Western consulting advice, particularly in areas such as corporate business strategy and structure (*World Executive's Digest*, 1997). The close-knit nature of senior management within the large family-owned *chaebol*, and their propensity for diversification on a scale unparalleled in the West, were very different from the companies Western consultancies typically advised.

Added to this, the *chaebol*'s selective use of external technical and managerial expertise and the focus on the internal generation of organizational learning also limited the demand for external management consulting services (Amsden, 1989: 269–90; Raymond & Rylance, 1996: 122). Where such services did exist these were invariably linked to domestic providers and the state's goal of targeted industry development. For instance the Korea Productivity Center, a non-profit institution founded in 1957, had a long history of national productivity promotion and proved an important conduit for the transmission of Japanese productivity improvement and quality management techniques in Korean industry from the 1960s (*Business Korea*, 1992; Korean Productivity Center, 2004). In this respect, the Korean experience seems similar to that of Japan and even Germany prior to the 1960s. As Kipping (2002) has argued in both of these economies, management knowledge diffusion occurred more readily through inter and intra-company cooperation and professional associations rather than via management consultancies.

By the early 1990s, a number of Korea's largest companies had begun to engage Western consultancies to advise on their corporate strategies and operations. Examples included the Lucky-Goldstar Group (LG) which hired McKinsey & Co., and Korea Telecom and Korea Explosives Group which used Monitor Consulting (management academic Michael Porter's consulting firm). Other Korean companies that used foreign consulting firms included Pohang Iron &

Steel Company (POSCO) and the Ssangyong Group (*Business Korea*, 1992). In 1991, following the government's relaxation of regulations on the operation of foreign service firms, McKinsey & Co. became the first Western management consultancy to establish a Korean office, with staff transferred from the firm's Tokyo office (McKinsey & Company, 2003a). McKinsey's rivals in the elite strategy consulting market, Boston Consulting Group (BCG) and Arthur D. Little followed similar paths and opened Seoul offices in 1994 focusing on corporate strategy, organizational change and operational efficiency (*Business Korea*, 2001; Arthur D. Little, 2003).

The other big players in the global management consulting market – the Big Six accounting firms – also established a Korean presence during this period. Typically this occurred through joint venture arrangements with local accountancy firms. For example in the early 1990s, Coopers & Lybrand formed a joint venture with the Samil Accounting Company, providing links to the global practice's consulting skills in operational efficiency and systems integration (*Business Korea*, 1998). As the managing partner of the local firm stated, 'to become internationally competitive and to create high added value, we are adopting the advanced management techniques of foreign firms and at the same time gaining experience in the Korean market' (*Business Korea*, 1998: 39). In a similar manner in 1997, another Western accounting major, Price Waterhouse bought into Consulting Software Group, Korea's largest independent consulting operation, employing 140 consultants who specialized in information systems implementation work. One of Price Waterhouse's first major Korean assignments was the implementation of an SAP information system for Samsung's entry into car manufacture (*Consultants News*, 1997; *Accounting Today*, 1997; Caldwell, 1997).

However, Korea proved to be a tough market for Western consultancies. Despite the removal of government restrictions on the establishment of local offices by foreign service providers, and the growing number of Korean managers with Western (typically US) management education, the distinctive nature of Korean economic development and the *chaebol's* tradition of internal innovation and organizational learning appeared antipathetic to Western concepts of external management experts and advisers. As one local management consultant bemoaned: Korean business managers 'don't' realize the importance of consulting, and they tend to try to solve their management problems themselves (*Business Korea*, 1992). By contrast, the unparalleled economic crisis of 1997 and the fundamental corporate restructuring that followed provided a far more favourable context for Western consultancies in their role as management fashion setters.

**The 1997 Economic Crisis and the Selling of Western 'Best Practice'**

The details of the 1997 Korean economic crisis and the economic reforms that followed have been extensively documented in a range of literature (Haggard, *et al.*, 2003; Kim, S.W., 2003; Kwack, 1999; Lee, 1999; Shin & Chang, 2003). The Korean Government's announcement in December 1997 that it was seeking financial assistance from the International Monetary Fund (IMF) came as a shock to international financial markets and precipitated a currency free-fall. Far from the earlier visions of an Asian miracle economy, Western financial analysts and the business press quickly ascribed blame for the crisis to fundamental structural weaknesses within the Korean economy. In particular, the *chaebol* became a key target of blame, accused of reckless investment decisions, inefficiency and corruption. The limitations of Korean management practice found popular expression in the Western business press which caricatured the Korean *chaebol* as inefficient expressions of a Confucian culture:

> Fortified by Korea's Confucian traditions that demand devotion to elders, Mr. Lee (Chairman of Samsung) and other captains of industry set almost unchallengeable agendas...The *chaebols* are often likened to Frankenstein's monster – very powerful, but inefficient and impossible to control (Baker, 1998).

Nor was this view limited to Western observers, with Korean government officials and bureaucrats also focusing on the *chaebol* as the source of the crisis. As one senior Korean economic adviser told a US newspaper, 'the families that control the *chaebol* are the ones responsible for bringing the country to such a mess' (cited in Beck, 1998: 1021). In return for the financial bail-out, the IMF demanded fundamental changes in macroeconomic policy, the liberalization of product and capital markets, changes in financial regulation, increased labour market flexibility, and the restructuring of the *chaebol* and their corporate governance structures, in short '...remoulding the Korean economy in the image of the (idealized) Anglo–American system' (Shin & Chang, 2003: 56). Nor were the *chaebol* in a position to challenge the reform agenda, facing public censure, financially constrained, and dealing with a new government determined to reform the conglomerates and restore Korea's credibility through high-profile reform measures. The restructuring of the *chaebol* involved debt reduction and attempts at lessening their levels of diversification, through what were known as the 'Big Deals' and 'Workout' programmes. The outcomes of this process involved a series of takeovers, mergers and bankruptcies (Shin and Chang, 2003: 84–102).

Dramatic economic change often provides a favourable environment for external advisers such as management consultants, as companies seek advice about how best to adapt to a new context, and anxious and uncertain managers look for quick solutions (Abrahamson, 1996; Gill & Whittle, 1993; Kieser, 1997). In the case of Korea, the extent and scale of the post-1997 economic reforms proved a boon to Western consultancies. The government's implementation of corporate restructuring and changes in corporate governance led to a frenzy of organizational change within large Korean companies. Implicit in this process was a government-endorsed rejection of the previous pattern of Korean economic development in favour of Western models of management. Western financial analysts and consultants reinforced this perception arguing that the economic crisis was an expression of the fundamental limitations of not only the Korean economic system, but also management practice within the *chaebol*.

For instance in 1998, the leading US management consultancy McKinsey & Co. published an influential report on the Korean economy that coincided with the worst of the economic crisis (McKinsey Global Institute, 1998). Through an analysis of eight key industries (steel, automotives, semiconductors, food, telecommunications, banking, retail and construction), the report argued that protectionism and poor corporate governance had resulted in inefficient management practices, and that productivity in many industries was less than 50 per cent of that of comparable US examples. For example, McKinsey noted that while Korea's car industry had invested in up-to-date technology, manufacturers had failed to adopt the lean production approach on a scale similar to that of best practice Japanese and American competitors. McKinsey claimed inefficient management and work practices, overstaffing, lack of a performance culture, and poor product and service mixes were also key impediments across other industries. In line with reform recommendations McKinsey had made in other countries (McKinsey Global Institute, 1995; 1997), the report argued the answer to Korea's economic woes was to lower barriers to imports and foreign direct investment and reform corporate governance, which would encourage competition, shareholder scrutiny and promote the diffusion of improved management practice. In particular, opening the economy to foreign firms and encouraging strategic partnerships with global 'best practice' companies was seen as a way in which Korean managers could quickly learn and adopt best management practices (McKinsey Global Institute, 1998: 7). A similar prognosis was provided by another US consultancy, A.T. Kearney, which argued that Korean industry lacked a sufficient focus on shareholder value and needed to embrace 'new skills and disciplines' such as 'dogged cost reduction', the outsourcing of non-core business, and joint ventures and strategic alliances with leading Western companies. The consultancy concluded:

> This shift in corporate behaviour is needed now in Korea if Korean industry is to compete successfully in the future. Those companies that make the shift now will win over those that do not (Turner, 2002).

Irrespective of whether senior managers accepted this criticism, it was clear that to appease external stakeholders such as the government, financial analysts and foreign investors, significant changes in the structure, strategy and internal operations of the *chaebol* were required. In this respect, engaging a prominent Western consulting firm could act as a powerful signalling device to external stakeholders that reform was in hand. Indeed, one senior client manager we interviewed, suggested that his Company's engagement of a Western consulting firm in the late 1990s for a series of restructuring projects was an outcome of direct government pressure. In addition to the knowledge and improved business practice that might be gained, engaging consultants could also provide a measure of certainty and security for Korean managers in a situation of unprecedented crisis and anxiety. Underlying both of these motivations was the fact that Western consultants were in demand because of their Western-ness; that is their primary appeal was their claims to be able to import Western business practice, which critics argued was essential for the survival of the Korean economy.

Western consultancies quickly positioned themselves as key agents in assisting Korean companies to implement 'best practice'. Consultancies with an established Korean presence were in the best position to take advantage of the sudden demand for consulting advice and quickly increased their staffing levels. For instance, from its initial staff of 2 partners and 17 consultants in the early 1990s, McKinsey's Seoul office had by 2002 grown to 8 partners and 110 consultants (McKinsey & Company, 2003a). Similarly, the consulting divisions of the large accounting firms also grew dramatically, with the newly merged Pricewaterhou-seCoopers by 2000 boasting over a thousand consultants in its Korean practice (Weber, 2000). The growing demand for Western consulting services also resulted in other consultancies entering the Korean market including A.T. Kearney and Bain & Co., as well as specialists in information technology such as Andersen Consulting and Deloitte Consulting (*Consultants News*, 1999).

Much of the post-crisis work of Western consultancies focused on the redesign of the *chaebol's* complex diversified business structures, the sale of non-core business units, and the introduction of a range of techniques, including process re-engineering, aimed at improving efficiency and productivity. American consultancy Arthur D. Little, for instance, produced reports on three of the so-called Big Deals outlining the restructuring of *chaebol* businesses in the semiconductor, petrochemical and oil refining industries (Arthur D. Little, 2003; Park, 1999). Demand was also particularly strong in the area of information technology, where the implementation of Enterprise Resource Planning (ERP) systems promised reduced cost through the integration of data and more efficient business processes (Caldwell, 1997; Davenport, 1998; Jang, *et al.*, 2002). Like the example of many Western companies during the 1990s, a key outcome of this corporate restructuring was organizational downsizing and delayering, resulting in major redundancies and job losses (Kim, W.B., 2003; Rowley & Bae, 2002: 540). Attempts by large Korean companies to introduce Western-style performance management systems and reduce the traditional reliance on seniority-based promotion and remuneration for white-collar and managerial employees (Pucik & Lim, 2002; Rowley & Bae, 2002), also led to a growth in human resource consulting.

The pervasiveness of Western consulting advice was highlighted by the role of Western consultants and investment banks in advising on the restructuring and sale of major financial institutions to foreign investors, and the rationalization of newly-privatized instrumentalities and government departments. For example, US advisers Morgan Stanley played a central role in advising the government over the sale of majority stakes in the Seoul Bank and Korea First Bank to foreign buyers. Western consultancies such as A.T. Kearney also gained major contracts with privatized instrumentalities such as SK Telecom and oversaw the outsourcing of business activities which it argued would result in significant cost savings. Kearney and other Western consultancies such as Andersen Consulting, Bain & Co. and Arthur Andersen also advised government departments such as Korea's Planning & Budget Commission on ways to cut costs, reduce staffing and implement new management systems and procedures (Clifford, 1999).

## Limits to Diffusion: Pragmatism and Resistance to Western Consulting

The growing demand for Western consultancies in the aftermath of the 1997 economic crisis appeared to reverse the traditional resistance of Korean business to external management consultants and led to the adoption of a range of Western management fashions such as re-engineering, downsizing, performance management and systems integration. However within the space of a few years, the demand for Western consulting services had receded, resulting in the closure of many Western consultancies (*The Electronic Times*, 2002). Several factors underpinned this reversal, in particular an unexpectedly rapid economic recovery, the perceived poor standard of consulting offerings, and the inability of many Western consultancies to transform their image as outsiders promoting Western solutions to Korean business.

Despite predictions of economic stagnation following the crisis, the Korean economy enjoyed a sharp recovery from late 1998, achieving a growth rate of 10.9 per cent in 1999. While advocates of economic reform claimed this turnaround as an outcome of the IMF programme, critics argued that the recovery resulted from traditional Korean government intervention and expansionary, Keynesian policies (Shin & Chang, 2003: 59–65). The rapidity of the economic turnaround and renewed success of companies such as Hyundai, Samsung and LG on global export markets undercut the post-crisis criticism of Korean management. Rather than corrupt and inefficient conglomerates, leading Korean companies were once again perceived as global corporations beating Western companies at their own game. The changed economic context also reduced the appeal of foreign consultancies importing Western 'best practice'. In this sense the image of foreign consultancies as outsiders while effective during the crisis period, was at best a short-term advantage within the Korean context.

Indeed, the gold rush of Western consultancies into Korea following the aftermath of the 1997 crisis resulted in an unsustainable number of consultancies and a poor level of service. Consultancies expanded rapidly during the later 1990s often by hiring young, local graduates who could be trained quickly and then sent out to work on consulting projects. A common theme in our interviews with senior *chaebol* managers was criticism of Western consultants both for the high cost of their services and the limited nature of their expertise. For instance, one senior manager expressed frustration with the Western consultants employed in his firm:

> Their skill, their knowledge was very much lower than myself. I had to teach them! They told us what we already knew, except their terminology was very good!

Indeed, consultants themselves acknowledged that the boom period of the late 1990s for consulting services led to dramatic and unsustainable growth.

> What actually happened I think is that everyone grew aggressively, hugely, including ourselves. There was a huge demand. In fact we ended up probably having 50 per cent of the people serving Korean clients coming from the rest of the world without necessarily growing our Korean base because at the time you couldn't find all of the talent. What's happened as the market has shrunk, we just pulled in a hell of a lot less from the outside.

As another consultant recollected:

> ...there were so many consulting firms, local and international and joint-venture ones with unacceptable quality. So it's now gone. All this unacceptable quality needed to be cleaned out.

Korean companies also proved to be discriminating consumers and resistant to the selling strategies of Western consultancies. Expatriate Western consultants viewed Korea as one of the toughest markets they had worked in, emphasizing the rigorous way in which clients assessed consulting proposals, offered projects to multiple consultancies even in cases of strong pre-existing client–consultant relationships, and viewed consultancy assignments in a far more transactional manner than typical American or Australian companies. Hence while leading *chaebol* would often use Western consultancies as a source of information and advice regarding their globalization strategies or benchmarking their performance against overseas competitors, they were less willing to extend these consulting relationships into the implementation of changed practice within their businesses. As the senior partner in one Western consultancy stated:

> I would call it an immature market. They're not as used to wanting to partner with us to go and achieve something. They want to take something from us and do it themselves...it's much more transaction driven.

In part this reflected the significant internal resources within the major Korean business groups. For instance, the traditional model within the *chaebol* of central Planning Departments and Research Institutes provided significant internal consulting resources. The adoption of integrated information technology systems also harnessed such traditions of internal knowledge generation and information sharing to a far greater extent than typical Western business organizations (Jang, *et al.*, 2002). As several consultants acknowledged in the areas of systems integration and ERP implementation, the *chaebol's* internal IT groups were often strong competitors given their insider status and lower price point. Where Western consultancies had succeeded in moving beyond the provision of advice and assisting in implementation projects, this often required partnership with such internal consultancies.

The changed economic context also highlighted limitations in the ability of Western consultancies to integrate themselves within the Korean business context. The global expansion of management consultancies often involved the development of connections with local business and social elites as a means of establishing legitimacy and tapping into local business networks as a source of new work (Kipping, 1999). Management consultancies have also sought to develop closer client relations as a means of generating greater repeat business (Kitay & Wright, 2004). However, such networking and local embeddedness takes time to develop, particularly in distinctive institutional and cultural contexts (Kipping, 2002). For Western providers of professional services, the Korean business context was especially difficult to break into given the strong emphasis placed on family and kinship ties, and school, university and military backgrounds (Raymond & Rylance, 1996: 113–4). As one expatriate consultant emphasized:

> Korean culture, where you went to school, how old you are and who you know is vital. Very important. If you've been to Seoul National University or Yonsei, the top couple of universities, that opens a lot of doors. It still fascinates me that you'll walk around and it's like (sic) "he went to my old school, he's three years difference to me, but I know he went there and we probably talked twice in the last 20 years but that's okay". That's a relationship that you can use and they'll acknowledge and respect. Now I can think of people that I went to school with three years difference from me and I wouldn't dare ring them up or do something like that.

Those consultancies which survived the shake-out in the industry were also the firms which most successfully localized their Korean operations. This involved highlighting Korean partners with specific local knowledge and business contacts, as well as the employment of a dominantly Korean workforce (Boston Consulting Group, 2000; McKinsey & Company, 2003b). Such localization presented a challenge to the one world model of Western consultancies which stressed their ability to fly in experienced consultants from around the world. As one consultant reflected:

> But one of the differences doing practice here, is I can't bring a team of people from overseas to do these jobs. It just doesn't work here because of the language particularly, and also the culture to some extent. For example in Australia if I was trying to build a practice there, if I went back 10 years, even to sell large pieces of work, you can bring 50 Americans or whatever to do it right, it works. You cannot do that here, it's impossible. The projects wouldn't survive, first from a cost basis, and secondly from a language basis, you just can't get the working relationships or the working knowledge going.

Finally, at the enterprise level, external consultants also faced significant resistance to attempts to change organizational structures and the prevailing business culture. The ability of external consultants to reform longstanding organizational practice is often limited and subject to resistance from line management and other employees (Kipping & Armbrüster, 2002; Wright, 2002). Media coverage of post-crisis restructuring commonly highlighted Western consultancies as the vanguard in the battle to change Korean business practice. As one article reported:

> Young, American-educated Koreans employed by foreign consultancies often find themselves in the front line of pulling down the old Confucian order. A *chaebol* office worker recounts consultants in their late twenties confronting managers in their forties: 'They have to literally yell at them and say No, you can't do it like this!' (Baker, 1998).

However, the impact of consultants was also constrained by the strength of pre-existing custom and practice and employee, trade union and managerial resistance to aspects of the reform agenda. In terms of redundancies and job losses, Rowley and Bae (2002: 540) note a variety of examples where strikes and managerial reticence resulted in the watering-down of previously announced job losses. In terms of the adoption of Western-style human resource policies such as performance management and the removal of seniority-based pay and job security, research suggests that Korean companies have adopted these practices to varying degrees (Rowley & Bae, 2002). Our interviews with senior *chaebol* managers revealed similar variations in the acceptance of Western 'best practice', with techniques such as performance pay tailored to fit local circumstance, and temporary employment the subject of sustained and heated industrial negotiation. While acknowledging these changes as necessary, Korean managers also questioned their efficacy. Reflecting on the recent implementation in his firm of a new human resource information system by a leading Western consultancy, one senior *chaebol* manager expressed frustration with the system's inability to accommodate the nuances of Korean employment relations:

> from our eyes it is not efficient. We have to follow the global system but not totally. It needs to be more Korean oriented.

## Discussion and Implications

Management consultancies are often portrayed as central actors within a growing management advice industry, involved in the creation, commodification and diffusion of various management fashions (Abrahamson, 1996; Kieser, 1997; Micklethwait & Wooldridge, 1996; Shapiro, 1996). Implicit within this vision is an assumption that fashion setters such as consultants often determine the form and nature of the knowledge exchange, with client managers as consumers seen as passive and sometimes gullible recipients. However, the role of consultants in the diffusion of management knowledge is invariably more complex than this stereotype presumes, with consultants subject to the insecurities of establishing and maintaining legitimacy, and client managers often acting as a sceptical and critical audience (Fincham, 1999; Sturdy, 1997).

The example of Korean business responses to Western management consulting highlights elements of both sides of this debate. On the one hand, the example of the 1997 economic crisis and the ability of Western consultancies to position themselves as key agents in the transfer of management best practice, supports aspects of the management fashion model of diffusion. In a period of unparalleled economic crisis, anxious and uncertain Korean managers eagerly embraced Western consultants given the prevailing interpretation among government and financial analysts that the crisis was an expression of the failings of Korean management. This was an interpretation that Western consultancies themselves emphasized through publications and media pronouncements, which publicized their own potential role in overcoming the crisis, particularly their ability to bring 'best practice' to their clients. From the perspective of *chaebol* managers, irrespective of their belief in the rational advantages that might flow from consultancy use, engaging Western consultants also served an important symbolic role; signalling to external stakeholders that change was occurring and superior Western practices were being adopted.

However, the apparent dominance of Western management consultants following the 1997 crisis was short-lived. The rapid and unexpected economic recovery undercut much of the rationale that Western consultancies had relied on. Hence, while their appeal as outside carriers of Western management knowledge proved a boon during the immediate aftermath of the crisis, once circumstances changed, the appeal of Western consultants as outsiders declined. In the Korean case this reflected the prevailing culture within large companies to focus on the internalization of management expertise (institutional innovation) and the close-knit nature of managerial networks based on familial and educational linkages. Foreign consultancies that survived the contraction in demand for consulting services, did so on the basis of aggressively localizing their operations by integrating within the Korean business community and employing a predominantly Korean workforce. Moreover, Western consultants also faced resistance from Korean managers, employees and trade unions to aspects of their change agendas which clashed with prevailing custom and practice (for example the downsizing and delayering of white-collar and managerial jobs). As a result, Korean managers exhibited a selective and pragmatic adoption of Western consulting advice, improvising and adapting Western management fashions to fit their organizations.

**Conclusion**

Our study demonstrates that the concept of management fashion while a useful construct in analysing management knowledge diffusion, needs to take greater account of the role of varying institutional, cultural and organizational contexts. Far from a one-way flow from fashion setter to fashion consumer, our study demonstrates how varying contexts can at different times both impede and assist management knowledge diffusion. Fashion setters such as consultants are far from free agents and are themselves dependent on the reactions of their consumer market. Managers and employees as consumers of management fashions, may well reject the attempts of foreign fashion setters to sell innovations that fail to fit with their business environment, or adopt such innovations in a pragmatic and creative manner (Gabriel, 2002). By contrast, in circumstances where local practice is seen as problematic, such alien innovations may be increasingly attractive simply because of their foreign nature.

Teasing out these shifting dynamics and the circumstances under which the diffusion process is affected, requires further research in divergent social and economic settings. The recent expansion of management consulting in other Asian economies, such as China and India, offer further potential arenas in which to study the role of consultancies in diffusing management ideas and practices. There is also a need for more company-level case studies of how management knowledge is created and packaged by global consultancies for new and developing markets, and correspondingly how such fashions are received, interpreted and adapted by individual businesses within these markets.

## Acknowledgements

The authors would like to thank the managers and consultants who participated in interviews. We are also grateful to the Editors and referees for their comments and suggestions on earlier drafts of this article. Financial support for this research project was provided by an Australian Research Council Discovery Grant (DP 0345473).

## References

Abrahamson, E. (1991) Managerial fads and fashions: the diffusion and rejection of innovations, *Academy of Management Review*, 16(3), pp. 586–612.

Abrahamson, E. (1996) Management fashion, *Academy of Management Review*, 21(1), pp. 254–285.

*Accounting Today* (1997) PW helps Samsung build cars, Jan. 6–19, p. 25.

Alvarez, J. (Ed.) (1998) *The Diffusion and Consumption of Business Knowledge* (Houndmills: Macmillan).

Amsden, A. H. (1989) *Asia's Next Giant: South Korea and Late Industrialization* (New York: Oxford University Press).

Arthur D. Little (2003) ADL Korea at a Glance, <http://www.adl.co.kr/english/seoul_history.html>, accessed 1 June 2004.

Baker, M. (1998) Out with Confucius in Korea's big firms, *Christian Science Monitor*, 11 March.

Beck, P. M. (1998) Revitalizing Korea's Chaebol, *Asian Survey*, 38(11), pp. 1018–1035.

Benders, J., van den Berg, R.J. & van Bijsterveld, M. (1998) Hitch-hiking on a hype: Dutch consultants engineering re-engineering, *Journal of Organizational Change Management*, 11(3), pp. 201–215.

Bessant, J. & Rush, H. (1995) Building bridges for innovation: the role of consultants in technology transfer, *Research Policy*, 24(1), pp. 97–114.

Boston Consulting Group (2000) BCG Seoul: People, <http://www.bcg.co.kr/people.html>, accessed 8 May 2004.

*Business Korea* (1992) Local firms after a piece of the action, *Business Korea*, June, pp. 38–39.

*Business Korea* (1998) Korea's largest consulting group, *Business Korea*, Jan., pp. 29–30.

*Business Korea* (2001) World leader in strategic consulting, *Business Korea*, June, p. 62.

Caldwell, B. (1997) Consulting goes global: Price Waterhouse inks overseas deals, *Information Week*, 17 March, pp. 100.

Child, J. (1981) Culture, contingency and capitalism in the cross-national study of organizations, in: L. L. Cummings & B. M. Staw (Eds) *Research in Organizational Behaviour*, pp. 303–356 (Greenwich, CT: JAI Publishers).

Child, J. & Rodrigues, S. (1996) The role of social identity in the international transfer of knowledge through joint ventures, in: S. Clegg & G. Palmer (Eds) *The Politics of Management Knowledge* (London: Sage).

Clark, T. (2004) The fashion of management fashion: a surge too far?, *Organization*, 11(2), pp. 297–306.

Clark, T. & Fincham, R. (Eds) (2002) *Critical Consulting: New Perspectives on the Management Advice Industry* (Oxford: Blackwell).

Clifford, M. (1999) Fetch me a Westerner: US consultants are thriving in Asia, *Business Week*, 8 March, p. 14.

*Consultants News* (1997) PW eyes South Korea, April, p. 3.

*Consultants News* (1999) Deloitte opens Seoul office, April, p. 3.

Davenport, T. (1998) Putting the enterprise into the enterprise system, *Harvard Business Review*, 76(4), pp. 121–131.

DiMaggio, P. & Powell, W. (1983) The iron cage revisited: institutional isomorphism and collective rationality in organizational fields, *American Sociological Review*, 48, April, pp. 147–160.

*Electronic Times, The* (2002) Multinational consulting firms – domestic SI industry forging collaboration, 20 Nov.

Ernst, D. (2001) Catching-up and postcrisis industrial upgrading: searching for new sources of growth in Korea's electronics industry, in: F. C. Deyo, R. F. Doner & E. Hershberg (Eds) *Economic Governance and the Challenge of Flexibility in East Asia*, pp. 137–164 (Lanham, MD: Rowman & Littlefield).

Fincham, R. (1999) The consultant-client relationship: critical perspectives on the management of organizational change, *Journal of Management Studies*, 36(3), pp. 335–351.

Gabriel, Y. (2002) Essai: on paragrammatic uses of organizational theory-a provocation, *Organization Studies*, 23(1), pp. 133–151.

Gill, J. & Whittle, S. (1993) Management by panacea: accounting for transience, *Journal of Management Studies*, 30(2), pp. 281–295.

Guillén, M. (1994) *Models of Management. Work, Authority, and Organization in a Comparative Perspective* (Chicago: The University of Chicago Press).

Guillén, M. (2001) Is globalization civilizing, destructive or feeble? a critique of five key debates in the social-science literature, *Annual Review of Sociology*, 27, pp. 235–260.

Guirdham, M. (1999) *Communicating Across Cultures*, W. Lafayette, IN: Ichor.

Haggard, S., Lim, W. & Kim, E. (Eds) (2003) *Economic Crisis and Corporate Restructuring in Korea: Reforming the Chaebol* (Cambridge: Cambridge University Press).

Hofstede, G. (1994) The business of international business is culture, *International Business Review*, 3(1), pp. 1–13.

Huczynski, A. (1993) Explaining the succession of management fads, *International Journal of Human Resource Management*, 4(2), pp. 443–463.

Jang, S., Hong, K., Bock, G. W. & Kim, I. (2002) Knowledge management and process innovation: the knowledge transformation path in Samsung SDI, *Journal of Knowledge Management*, 6(5), pp. 479–485.

Khanna, T. & Palepu, K. (1999) The right way to restructure conglomerates in emerging markets, *Harvard Business Review*, 77(4), pp. 125–134.

Kieser, A. (1997) Rhetoric and Myth in Management Fashion, *Organization*, 4(1), pp. 49–74.

Kim, L. (1997) *Imitation to Innovation: The Dynamics of Korea's Technological Learning* (Boston: Harvard Business School Press).

Kim, S. W. (2003) Should Business Groups Be Blamed for the Asian Financial Crisis? Evidence from South Korea, *Asia Pacific Business Review*, 9(3), pp. 1–20.

Kim, W. B. (2003) Economic Crisis, Downsizing and 'Layoff Survivors Syndrome', *Journal of Contemporary Asia*, 33(4), pp. 449–464.

Kipping, M. (1999) American management consulting companies in Western Europe, 1910s to 1990s: products, reputation, and relationships, *Business History Review*, 73(2), pp. 190–220.

Kipping, M. (2002) Why management consulting developed so late in Japan and does it matter?, *Hitotsubashi Business Review*, 50(2), pp. 6–21.

Kipping, M. & Armbrüster, T. (2002) The burden of otherness: limits of consultancy interventions in historical case studies, in: M. Kipping & L. Engwall (Eds) *Management Consulting: Emergence and Dynamics of a Knowledge Industry* (Oxford: Oxford University Press).

Kipping, M. & Engwall, L. (Eds) (2002) *Management Consulting: Emergence and Dynamics of a Knowledge Industry* (Oxford: Oxford University Press).

Kitay, J. & Wright, C. (2004) Take the money and run? Organisational boundaries and consultants roles, *The Service Industries Journal*, 24(3), pp. 1–18.

Koo, H. (2001) *Korean Workers: The Culture and Politics of Class Formation* (Ithaca: NY: Cornell University Press).

Korean Productivity Center (2004) *KPC and Productivity Movement* (Seoul: KPC).

Kostera, M. (1995) The modern crusade: the missionaries of management come to eastern Europe, *Management Learning*, 26(3), pp. 331–352.

Kostova, T. & Roth, K. (2002) Adoption of an organizational practice by subsidiaries of MNCs: institutional and relational effects, *Academy of Management Journal*, 45(1), pp. 215–233.

Kwack, S. Y. (1999) Korea's financial crisis: causes and restructuring tasks, *Multinational Business Review*, 7(2), pp. 55–59.

Kwon, S. H. & O'Donnell, M. (2001) *The Chaebol and Labour in Korea: The Development of Management Strategy in Hyundai* (London: Routledge).

Lee, J. W. (1999) Corporate Restructuring in Korea: Experience and Lessons, *Korea Journal*, 39(3), pp. 230–270.

Littler, C. (1982) *The Development of the Labour Process in Capitalist Societies: a Comparative Analysis of Work Organisation in Britain, the USA, and Japan* (London: Heinemann).

McKinsey & Company (2003a) The Seoul Office, <http://www.mckinsey.co.kr/seoul/seoul3_4.html>, accessed 8 May 2004.

McKinsey & Company (2003b) McKinsey Seoul: Our People, <http://www.mckinsey.co.kr/people/people4_0.html>, accessed 8 May 2004.

McKinsey Global Institute (1995) *Sweden's Economic Performance* (Stockholm: McKinsey & Co).

McKinsey Global Institute (1997) *Removing Barriers to Growth in France and Germany* (Frankfurt: McKinsey & Co).

McKinsey Global Institute (1998) *Productivity-Led Growth for Korea* (Seoul: McKinsey & Co).

Micklethwait, J. & Wooldridge, A. (1996) *The Witch Doctors: What the Management Gurus Are Saying, Why It Matters and How to Make Sense of It* (London: Heinemann).

Micklethwait, J. & Wooldridge, A. (2003) *A Future Perfect: The Challenge and Promise of Globalization* (New York: Random House).

Morris, T. (2000) From Key Advice to Execution? Consulting Firms and the Implementation of Strategic Decisions, in: P. Flood, T. Dromgoole, S. Carroll & L. Gorman (Eds) *Managing Strategic Implementation: An Organizational Behaviour Perspective*, pp. 125–137 (Oxford: Blackwell).

O'Shea, J. & Madigan, C. (1997) *Dangerous Company: The Consulting Powerhouses and the Businesses They Save and Ruin* (New York: Times Business).

Park, J. S. (1999) LG pulls out of chip business, *News From Asia–Pacific*, March, < http://www.nikkeibp.com/nea/mar99/napmar/korea.html > , accessed 18 May 2004.

Pucik, V. & Lim, J. C. (2002) Transforming HRM in a Korean *Chaebol*: a case study of Samsung, in: C. Rowley, T. W. Sohn & J. Bae (Eds) *Managing Korean Businesses: Organization, Culture, Human Resources and Change*, pp. 137–160 (London: Frank Cass).

Raymond, M. & Rylance, A. (1996) Evaluation and management of professional services in Korea, *Advances in International Marketing*, 7, pp. 111–125.

Rowley, C. & Bae, J. (2002) Globalisation and transformation of HRM in South Korea, *International Journal of Human Resource Management*, 13(3), pp. 522–549.

Shapiro, E. (1996) *Fad Surfing in the Boardroom: Managing in the Age of Instant Answers* (Reading, MA: Addison-Wesley).

Shin, J.-S. & Chang, H.-J. (2003) *Restructuring Korea Inc.: Financial Crisis, Corporate Reform, and Institutional Transition* (London: Routledge-Curzon).

Smith, C. & Meiskins, P. (1995) System, society and dominance effects in cross-national organisational analysis, *Work, Employment and Society*, 9(2), pp. 241–267.

Strange, S. (1997) The future of global capitalism; or will divergence persist forever?, in: C. Crouch & W. Streeck (Eds) *Political Economy of Modern Capitalism: Mapping Convergence and Diversity*, pp. 182–191 (London: Sage).

Sturdy, A. (1997) The consultancy process – an insecure business?, *Journal of Management Studies*, 34(3), pp. 389–413.

Sturdy, A. (2004) The adoption of management ideas and practices: theoretical perspectives and possibilities, *Management Learning*, 35(2), pp. 153–177.

Sturdy, A. & Gabriel, Y. (2000) Missionaries, mercenaries or car salesmen? MBA teaching in Malaysia, *Journal of Management Studies*, 37(7), pp. 979–1002.

Tsutsui, W. (1998) *Manufacturing Ideology: Scientific Management in Twentieth Century Japan* (Princeton, NJ: Princeton University Press).

Turner, W. (2002) Turning the corner on managing for profitability, *The Korea Times*, 3 Jan.

Weber, A. (2000) PwC CEO embracing risk to stay ahead, *Korea Herald*, 9 Sept.

Werr, A., Stjernberg, T. & Docherty, P. (1997) The functions of methods of change in management consulting, *Journal of Organizational Change Management*, 10(4), pp. 288–307.

Westney, D. E. (1987) *Imitation and Innovation: the Transfer of Western Organizational Patterns to Meiji Japan* (Cambridge, MA: Harvard University Press).

Whitley, R. (1999) *Divergent Capitalisms: The Social Structuring and Change of Business Systems* (Oxford: Oxford University Press).

*World Executive's Digest* (1997) The Threat of Fads: Asia's Antidotes, (July), p. 20

Wright, C. (2002) Promoting demand, gaining legitimacy and broadening expertise: the evolution of consultancy–client relationships in Australia, in: M. Kipping & L. Engwall (Eds) *Management Consulting: Emergence and Dynamics of a Knowledge Industry*, pp. 184–202 (Oxford: Oxford University Press).

Wright, C. & Kitay, J. (2004) Spreading the word: gurus, consultants and the diffusion of the employee relations paradigm in Australia, *Management Learning*, 35(3), pp. 271–286.

# Labour–Intensive Industrialization in Hong Kong, 1950–70: A Note on Sources and Methods

DAVID CLAYTON

## Introduction

Hong Kong was a small city-state whose economy was traditionally reliant on tertiary trades, such as shipping and financial services. It industrialized in the twentieth century, as did other parts of China, where a large proportion of world production of consumer goods (such as clothing, footwear and electronics) is now located. Although there are parallels between industrialization in Hong Kong and the current process of structural change in contemporary China, these can only be drawn imprecisely because historians have not had the necessary raw materials: written sources documenting Hong Kong's industrial past. Published time-series data is limited and unreliable, and, as shown here, fails to reveal an important feature of industrialization in Hong Kong: the existence, alongside factories, of numerous small workshops. New macro and survey data derived from archival sources allows a partial and patchy reconstruction of a more realistic (that is, dualistic) industrial landscape. These findings set up a larger project on 'Industrialization and Institutional Change in Hong Kong' (funded by the Leverhulme Trust), which sets out to analyse how businesses were affected by, and helped shape, legal and customary frameworks regulating industrial employment, the use of intellectual property rights, and access to overseas markets.

## Literature Review

The study of industrialization in Hong Kong divides into two schools of thought. One, that could be labelled the 'displacement' thesis, argues that industrialization was sudden, occurring between the late 1930s and the early 1950s, and caused by the transfer of capital, machinery and skilled labour from industrial areas in a war-torn and soon-to-be communist China (Wong, 1988; Riedel, 1974; Szcepanik, 1958). Capital-intensive modes of production (using centrally-powered machinery and semi-skilled labour) generated economic growth by mass-producing consumer goods, exported to Western, high-income markets. Hong Kong-based merchants (Braga, 1957), large Western retailers and overseas manufacturers sourced goods in, or sub-contracted production to, Hong Kong (Lee, 1999: 162–180; Meyer, 2000). A revisionist view, that could be labelled the 'evolutionary' thesis, argues that structural change occurred more gradually, dating back pre-war (Benham, 1956; Leeming, 1975). This debate has not been resolved due to deficiency of data for the study of Hong Kong's industrial history.

Macro-economic data sources for Hong Kong during the early to mid-twentieth century are poor. Neither the colonial government nor trade associations (Ngo, 1999: 123–6) collected standard, time-series data on industrial output, the empirical foundation stones on which economic historians reconstruct industrial pasts. More frustratingly, even though industries in Hong Kong relied on imports of raw materials and capital goods, and exported the vast majority of finished products, trade returns are inadequate substitutes. The government did not differentiate between exports and re-exports until after 1959, and so it is not possible to track precisely a process of import-substitution industrialization: although evidence exists that exports of industrial goods rose, this may merely indicate that local merchants were re-exporting goods made in Japan or elsewhere in China.

Micro-economic data is also highly deficient for Hong Kong. There is no data on production within households, which may have been of some significance during the early stages of industrialization. Furthermore, as most manufacturing took place in small firms with informal structures, which relied on the 'invisible hand' of the market, few written records were created. The vast majority of firms that kept records would have destroyed them, when they went bankrupt, when they relocated, or when the cost of storing paper under tropical climatic conditions and in a place where rents were high became prohibitive. An excellent oral history has filled the gap somewhat for the cotton textile industry, or rather for the large-scale, capital-intensive parts of it (Wong, 1988). There are also some useful surveys of management strategies (Epsy, 1974), and business histories of particular firms (Choi, 1988; Clayton, 2000i). However, we still know very little about labour-intensive modes of production.

## Theory

The existence within an industrializing Hong Kong of labour-intensive units of production, defined as ones that did not use power-driven machinery, is not surprising because during the twentieth century organizational, dualism (the differential use of technologies within society) was a common feature in developing economies (Thirlwall, 1994:128–29). In urban and rural areas clothing, furniture, shoes, toys, brooms, brushes and umbrellas, and other cheap consumer goods, were made by hand within households and in small workshops. Moreover, even in many developed parts of the world, labour (and knowledge) intensive production techniques successfully competed with capital-intensive ones. A growing body of evidence has encouraged scholars to critique the 'big business' framework put together by Alfred Chandler: they have argued that 'flexible' modes of production can compete with mass production (Sabel & Zeitlin, 1997).

There is evidence that craft-based industries, which had a long history in Asia, survived the twin impact of globalization and imperialism in the nineteenth and early twentieth centuries (Roy, 1993; 1999; Sugihara, 2003, 2004). Demand-side forces might in part explain their durability. Where the tastes of consumers continued to be shaped by culture, demand for 'traditional', hand-made products may have held-up, making it difficult for foreign and modern Asian-made products to take higher market shares. Supply-side forces, however, were probably of greater significance. Extensive and durable social networks, based on kinship and extra-kinships linkages, may have allowed small units of production to generate external economies of scale and minimize the transaction costs incurred when mobilizing capital, labour and raw materials, and when marketing finished products (Hamilton, 1996; Brown, 1996; Redding, 1990). Rapid urbanization also may have allowed small-scale firms to cluster into districts, so allowing them to generate further external economies of scale. In addition, from the end of the nineteenth century, small workshops could use small, portable, electric and petrol-driven motors, the adoption of which blurred the distinction between labour and capital-intensive modes of production.

## Research Questions

Will a reconstructed industrial landscape for Hong Kong reveal that small, labour-intensive workshops existed alongside capital-intensive factories?

If so, how will the new evidence re-shape the 'evolutionary' and the 'displacement' theses used to frame the study of Hong Kong's industrial history; and can it help to inform theories about the evolution of labour-intensive industrialization?

## Data Analysis

The only standard time-series data that exists (for the post-war period only) is on industrial employment. To regulate factory conditions, a Labour department was set up early in the post-war period and it registered and periodically inspected factories (England & Rear, 1975: 53–59). It published annual reports, which chronicled the growth of industrial employment. The data in these reports has been used to show that the average size of units of production fell steadily post-war; from 55 employees per establishment in 1950, to 42 in 1960, and to 33 in

1970 (Yu, 1997: 71). These measurements are crude, and the findings misleading, because the data is highly deficient.

Enterprises were only subject to inspection and thus registration if they employed more than twenty workers; used power-driven or dangerous machinery; or employed women and young people. Consequently, organizational dualism is not revealed in the published data. A 1962 report by the Economist Intelligence Unit (EIU), one commissioned by the organized business community, recognized that the existing data was deficient; that the Labour Department statistics were 'biased in favour of certain of the more highly-mechanized industries, notably spinning and cotton weaving, and the metal and engineering industries' (EIU, 1962: 5). In 1952, the Hong Kong administration estimated (privately) that 50,000 people were employed in 'cottage industry and small industrial undertakings' as compared with 100,000 in registered ones; by 1957, the government estimated that registered enterprises employed 150,000, unregistered ones 100,000.[1] Many of these firms were illicit, evading factory inspectors even though they were using power-driven machinery. Many were licit: they did not have to register because they were small and used traditional, labour-intensive production techniques.

There is an alternative, non-published, source that recorded employment in some (but, unfortunately not all) labour-intensive units. During the 1950s, the Commerce and Industry Department provided firms with export licences and disseminated information on Hong Kong-based manufacturers to those wanting to sell Hong Kong-made goods in overseas markets (Clayton, 2000ii). All industrial enterprises – whether they were 'factories' or 'workshops' – had to acquire import and export licences from this department if they wanted to export to the UK, British Commonwealth and Empire markets, and to the USA, the most significant markets for Hong Kong exports. Consequently, the Department of Commerce and Industry recorded 2000 more 'undertakings' than the 5000 registered with the Labour Department (EIU, 1962: 5–6). There was a 'further 2,000' firms, which were not registered with the Labour Department or with the Commerce and Industry Department but they only sold products within Hong Kong, not overseas (EIU, 1962: 5–6). So in total, there may have been as many as 4,000 small workshops in late 1950s Hong Kong, of which a half were able to compete in international markets.

Raw data, discovered in the archives of the Commerce and Industry Department, survives for 349 enterprises registering to be accredited suppliers between 1955–58, a period of particularly rapid industrial growth. The data comprises a five per cent sample of the 7,000 industrial enterprises that the EIU listed as exporting goods overseas; a 4 per cent sample of the 9000 firms engaged in industrial production for home and overseas markets. (However the sample size is likely to be larger as it is being compared with benchmark data for a slightly later period, the early 1960s, by which stage the manufacturing sector was much larger.) This is, then, a good-sized sample. However, it does not differentiate between labour and capital-intensive units of production. It would have included both sorts. It is, also, likely to be a slightly skewed sample, over representing small firms, and thus perhaps workshops.

Manufacturers would have had an incentive to register because by establishing direct contact with, say, large-scale retailers and wholesalers based overseas, they could circumvent export houses in Hong Kong and thus potentially reap higher mark-ups. But longer-established firms would have registered before 1955–58, and they should, in theory, have been larger than new entrants into the market registering between 1955–58. The archival record lists 191 factories as having been registered in August, September, October, November and December 1955; 114 in May and July 1957; and 44 in July of 1958. It does not indicate when, precisely, this scheme for the accreditation of enterprises was established but it probably dated back to the early 1950s when bureaucratic controls were imposed on exports to the USA (Clayton, 1997: 109–111).

Table 1 describes the distribution of employment in the sample data, and not unsurprisingly, it shows that a higher proportion of firms were small, employing under 50 employees. As a result, it confirms that the Labour Department data overestimates the average size of units of production in the late 1950s, and underestimates the number of people working in small workshops; the sample data shows that 26 per cent of people worked in enterprises employing less than 20 employees, compared with only 13 per cent in the Labour Department data. If, moreover, the distribution of industrial employment by firm size is compared with the more reliable and representative industrial censuses undertaken in the 1970s and 1980s, the best fit for firms employing fewer than 20 employees is between the sample data and the census data. This suggests that the average unit of production did not change during industrialization in Hong Kong, and that throughout the period a quarter of the industrial workforce was employed in small workshops.

The data can be disaggregated for 272 of the enterprises, and unsurprisingly, as shown in Table 2 enterprises making apparel, footwear and miscellaneous light industrial goods, where labour-intensive modes of production were common, were

**Table 1.** Employment in factories

| Range | Number of enterprises | Number employed | Percentage employed | Percentage employed 1955–58* | Percentage employed 1970s– 1980s** |
|---|---|---|---|---|---|
| 1–19 | 210 | 2242 | 26 | 12.8 | 22 |
| 20–49 | 111 | 3267 | 38 | 17.2 | 16.7 |
| 50–99 | 17 | 1370 | 16 | 13.5 | 16 |
| 100–199 | 7 | 1248 | 14.6 | 13.2 | 14.1 |
| 200–499 | 1 | 410 | 4.8 | 18.8 | 14.1 |
| 500–999 | 0 | - | | 10.2 | 8.4 |
| Over 1000 | 0 | - | | 13.8 | 8.5 |

*Sources:* Public Record Office, Hong Kong, TD3141/3665/52: list of factories registered in Trade Development Division [of the Commerce and Industry Department].

*The Annual Reports of the Commissioners of Labour, various years, 1950–1965, PRO, UK, CO131.

** data derived from 1978 and 1985 *Survey of Industrial Production*, Census and Statistics Department, Hong Kong, as cited in Edward K. Y. Chen and Kui-Wai Li, 'Industry', in H. C. Y. Ho and L. C. Chau, *The Economic System of Hong Kong*, Hong Kong, 1988, p. 114.

**Table 2.** Factory size (By number of employees)

| (Number of factories in brackets) | Average size | Average size (Department of Labour data) |
|---|---|---|
| Textiles (54) | 50 | 64 |
| Apparel & footwear (77) | 40 | 48 |
| Metal products (22) | 41 | 54 |
| Miscellaneous (33) | 22 | 31 |

*Sources:* As in Table 1.

small. The sample also provides a crude guide to how labour and machinery was used. Table 3 shows that most workers in enterprises employing fewer than 20 workers used machinery, whereas there were fewer machines per person in larger factories. This is because in larger plants semi-skilled workers were employed on a shift basis, and operated complex, centrally power-driven machinery. In many small enterprises, skilled and semi-skilled workers would have used hand-held, traditional implements, plus battery and petrol-powered machinery. The evidence shown in Table 4 is more clear-cut: textile and metalwork trades were more capital-intensive, while clothing and miscellaneous industries were more labour-intensive.

These are useful, corrective, findings. However, they fail to show how labour-intensive and capital-intensive firms interacted, and do not demonstrate that labour-intensive production methods survived during the 1960s and 1970s. By then labour was becoming scarce and wages were rising, so capital-labour ratios should have been changing in response. Survey data on two labour-intensive industries begins to fill this empirical gap. The study of the rattanware furniture and basket industry shows how labour and capital-intensive units of production co-existed in the same sector. The study of the umbrella industry shows how even though production became concentrated into larger, integrated units, dualism continued to characterize this particular sector to 1970.These industries were chosen because they had a long history in Hong Kong, and because their evolution in the 1950s and 1960s can be reconstructed from a range of documents derived from three separate sources:

1.  From the 1940s, labour officers working in the Labour Department investigated certain service and manufacturing sectors. Brief reports survive

**Table 3.** Labour-machinery ratio (By factory size)

| Range | Labour to machinery ratio |
|---|---|
| 1–19 | 1: 0.9 |
| 20–49 | 1: 0.6 |
| 50–99 | 1: 0.9 |
| 100–199 | 1: 0.5 |
| 200–499 | - |
| 500–999 | - |
| Over 1000 | - |

*Sources:* As in Table 1.

**Table 4.** Labour-machinery ratios (by sectors)

| Industry | Labour: machine ratio |
| --- | --- |
| Textiles (ISIC group 23) | 1: 1.3 |
| Wearing apparel and footwear (group 24) | 1: 0.8 |
| Metal products, except machinery and transport equipment (group 35) | 1: 1.3 |
| Miscellaneous manufacturing industries (group 39) | 1: 0.5 |

*Sources:* As in Table 1.

on the rattanware, umbrella and embroidery industries. These reports are based on interviews with employers and workers, and on written evidence submitted by trade unions and trade associations. They were commissioned because two of these trades (rattan, and embroidery) were in decline, characterized by high levels of unemployment, and the third (umbrella-making) had a long history of industrial unrest. Although, they focus on industrial relations, they include background information on industrial organization.

2.   From the mid 1960s, in response to the rise of protectionism overseas (epitomized by the Short and Long Term Arrangements at the GATT, which codified the use of voluntary export restraints and quotas), the Hong Kong government encouraged manufacturers to raise productivity and improve the quality of Hong Kong-made products (Nthenda, 1979: 167–183). A Trade and Industry Advisory Board (comprising members from the main chambers of commerce and representatives from the Commerce and Industry Department) commissioned reports on the umbrella, steel, electronics, enamelware, electric bulbs, and glove industries. These contain information on capital investments as well as employment.

3.   During the 1950s, when exports of particular products to the US rose quickly (as in the case of rattanware) or when particular sectors (such as plastics) imported raw and semi-processed inputs from the USA, American consuls in Hong Kong investigated Hong Kong industries, and wrote reports that survive in the US National Archives.

The rattan furniture and basket ware sector, which in Hong Kong had a history dating back to the early twentieth century, was, by the 1950s employing between 15,000 and 30,000 people making goods exported to high-income Western markets, notably the USA which imported between 60 and 80 per cent of local output.[2] Production was not integrated, as this was 'largely a handicraft', 'home industry type-operation'. Overseas orders for rattan furniture were received by export houses or by 'manufacturer–collectors' who had the capital to pay for warehousing and to provide suppliers with credit; four of them, all family firms, conducted 75 per cent of the export business. Production was usually sub-contracted to a range of workshops. These small workshops employing between 5 and 75 workers bought semi-processed inputs from three 'relatively large firms' producing 'machine-made rattan peel and core', or from import merchants. Exporters or 'manufacturer-collectors' finished off, sorted and stored goods, before they were shipped. To ensure high standards of workmanship and to prevent new designs being copied, the production of more specialist and innovative goods was undertaken in-house by 'manufacturer-collectors'. At the other end of the spectrum, products 'in continuous demand' (such as basket ware and 'saucer chairs'), and thus less subject to design shifts, were made by 'independent [home] workers'; they used their own capital to buy tools and raw materials, selling finished products to 'manufacturer collectors'. There were, however, relatively few independent artisans, as most people worked in small workshops.

In 1962 there were 47 enterprises making umbrella and umbrella parts, employing c.400 people, divided between larger, more capital-intensive units of production and smaller, labour-intensive ones, with five large factories specializing in the production of ribs (the most capital-intensive component of the process) and employing three quarters of the workforce. By 1970, the industry had grown to 77 enterprises employing 2,370, and the average size of each plant had risen four-fold.[3] But 80 per cent of enterprises still employed fewer than 50 workers. By then six firms had integrated all of the five production processes, cutting, sewing, frame-making, mounting and finishing, and it was probably these larger manufacturers, plus well-established merchants, that co-ordinated economic activities across the sector. In the 1950s, nine merchant houses dominated the export business, and, even by 1970, only 18 manufacturing firms had any capacity to sell directly, and only three survived without taking orders from merchants or from large-scale, integrated manufacturers.

Dualism remained a defining characteristic within the umbrella industry even in the 1960s due to the low cost of entering and exiting the market. As in many labour-intensive sectors, the vast majority of enterprises (90 per cent in 1970) were located in rented domestic premises rather than in purpose-built units; indeed, in 1970 for the sector as a whole factory overhead costs comprised on average only seven per cent of total costs of production. Entrepreneurs did not need to pay for expensive equipment. Fixed costs per worker were low, in 1970 HK$656 compared to an average for local light industry of HK$2,500–3,500. Moreover, as labour laws were poorly developed, workers could be easily dismissed, and machinery for cutting and sewing cloth could, if orders fell, be reused to produce different goods or sold. With expenditure on land, labour and capital low, 70 per cent of production costs went on buying materials (raw and semi-processed). During boom times, contractors and merchants may have provided credit to cover these costs. Demand, not supply-side factors, therefore, determined entry into and exit from the market, and, as a result, in this particular trade, capital and labour were highly mobile factors of production; of the 77 enterprises recorded in 1970, only 26 had existed in the 1950s, and nearly half were less than five years old.

## Discussion

It is evident that published data on industrial employment is unreliable. For the 1950s, it underestimates industrial employment; exaggerates the average size of units of production; and does not reveal organizational dualism. Conducting long run, time-series analysis of this data is highly problematic: before it is undertaken we need a better understanding on how methods of data collection shifted over time. It is already known that by mid 1960s, the Labour Department was recording an estimated 63 per cent of manufacturing employment, and by 1973, a few years before the first industrial census, 93 per cent (Riedel, 1974: 73, 93; Young, 1989: 236–7). New archival evidence presented here has shown that by 1957 the Labour Department was recording an estimated 60 per cent of industrial employment (150,000 workers out of an estimated total workforce of 250,000). As the colonial government was well aware that its data on industrial employment was deficient, why did it not collect better time-series data on industrial employment in the 1950s?

During the epoch of rapid industrialization, the population of Hong Kong rose quickly, mainly due to mass immigration from a war-torn and revolutionary China. Understandably, the colonial administration gave priority to raising employment levels, and decided not to regulate the manufacturing sector stringently, as this might have increased the cost of employing labour and reduced the competitiveness of Hong Kong exports. In the early 1950s, a labour officer admitted that:

> ...many factories... were well established by the time we learned of their existence. At this time commerce was flagging, and industry, once the small boy of the family, was developing into the breadwinner. The policy adopted was to consider first the all round economy of the Colony, and not to break rice bowls if it could be avoided.[4]

This in part explains why, despite the pace of industrialization, the government was slow to recruit more factory inspectors (Clayton, forthcoming ). From the mid 1950s, as the colonial administration came under international pressure to alleviate 'sweatshop' working conditions in the colony, this policy shifted, and the state, working with the organized business community, registered more industrial enterprises; and sought to raise industrial productivity, in part by encouraging small firms to relocate to purpose-built factory units with access to a supply of mains electricity. But this new policy was, from the outset, to be implemented gradually: 'discipline' was to be applied without imposing 'undue hardship upon the thousands of small traders, home industries, and 'shoestring' workshops.[5] It also took many years to recruit and train more inspectors, who had to be multi-lingual (able to communicate in many dialects of Chinese and in English) and, in an environment known for petty corruption, trustworthy.

The new (but still piecemeal) sources show that there were thousands of 'shoestring' workshops in 1950s Hong Kong. Also known by contemporaries as 'mushroom' enterprises – due to their ability to sprout up almost overnight – they employed a large number of people (up to 100,000 by the late 1950s). As Hong Kong had a small domestic market (3 million people by 1960), and as trade in manufactured goods between Hong Kong and its main pre-war market China had declined for political reasons, most of these small enterprises would have sold their finished products to overseas markets in South East Asia and in the West. They survived therefore during a period of globalization – characterized by the integration of product markets. How then were such small labour-intensive firms able to compete with large, capital-intensive units of production?

This colonial city-state, with a small rural hinterland, experienced in the early post-war period a five-fold increase in population, from 600,000 in 1946 to 3 million in 1960. (Podmore, 1971: 21–55). A high proportion (over one million) of these new inhabitants of this increasingly densely populated place were recent migrants. Divorced from their ties to the land, and unable or unwilling to return to China-proper, they survived in their new home by selling their labour for food, shelter and, ultimately, luxuries, such as consumer durables (Clayton, 2004). Most worked in 'informal' sectors: in services (such as rickshaw pulling; the restaurant trade), and in manufacturing. A small proportion of recent migrants set up small-scale businesses. They used kinship networks to accumulate capital and to recruit and train labour. Many of these enterprises assembled, finished and packed-up light consumer goods, such as food, clothing and miscellaneous products such as toys and toothbrushes. As land was scarce, and rents high, many of these businesses were set-up within overcrowded pre-war tenements or on land occupied by squatters. Most did not register with the state, nor adhere to any government regulations (on employment; and health and safety). They operated, precariously, in the 'extra-legal' sector.

These entrepreneurs suffered from extremely insecure property rights of the sort that hamstrung business ventures in other cities in the developing world (de Soto, 2000). To survive they entered and exited markets quickly, and kept capital–labour ratios low. By remaining small in scale, and limited in scope, they became entrepreneurial: they used simple machinery and knowledge that could be transferred to alternative uses; they did not integrate horizontally or vertically to generate economies of scale (Chandler, 1990), but instead generated external economies of scale by using markets or networks to establish ties with other producers and distributors at different stage of the production cycle; they responded to price shifts by making semi-skilled workers unemployed, or by encouraging employees to work for longer to complete orders.

## Implications

Some of the pre-requisites for this form of labour-intensive industrialization in Hong Kong existed pre-war: an abundant supply of labour, strong social and urban networks. However, unlike in the post-war period, product markets across the world were less open and global income levels lower. Moreover, post-war, small labour-intensive units in Hong Kong would not have faced such strong competition from handicraft producers elsewhere in China-proper. In Taiwan and Communist China, post-war governments adopted policies (such as import–substitution–industrialization; and economic planning) that discriminated against labour-intensive industries. Important demand-side pre-requisites for the expansion of labour-industrialization in Hong Kong may therefore have been missing until the post-war period. Moreover, extremely rapid population growth depressed wages in 1950s Hong Kong (Chow, 1977), and this would have made it far easier for firms using labour-intensive techniques to compete in international markets. The debate about the timing of industrialization in Hong Kong remains unresolved: the new evidence does not support exclusively either of the frameworks ('evolutionary' and 'displacement') used to tell the story of industrialization in Hong Kong.

These piecemeal sources, by demonstrating that 'labour-intensive' units of production existed during the epoch of rapid industrialization in Hong Kong, add to a body of evidence that shows that production in small workshops and within households survived in an industrializing Asia, and, significantly, in a part of it that was by the 1950s integrated into global markets for manufactured goods. Historians must therefore find out more about such industries. Ideally we need to know how much output labour-intensive industries contributed relative to capital-intensive ones in 1950s Hong Kong; and whether labour-intensive industrialization was a viable alternative to capital-intensive, mass production, over the longer term, into the 1960s and 1970s.

Labour-intensive units were probably much more important in terms of employment than output. As wages rose from the late 1950s, employment in labour-intensive pursuits should have declined. Can new data be found to prove or disapprove these hunches? New sources will hopefully also tell us about the role of women in labour-intensive units production, a major empirical gap at present because women formed a large part of the industrial workforce in twentieth century Asia (Cheng and Hsiung, 1998). Labour-intensive industries could have employed women in-house or sub-contracted production processes to outworkers, so we need to know more about local labour markets for women's work. How, in particular, did households calculate the trade-offs: higher and more stable sources of income for the household; but lower levels of fertility, and, for women (but not necessarily for men), less discretionary time?

To establish firmer chronologies, and to enrich our understanding of labour-intensive industrialization, historians will need to uncover additional sources on production at the level of the firm and, if possible, the household. Other foreign governments (notably the Japanese) would have collected data on industrial organization in Hong Kong; so would non-government organizations (such as trade unions and trade associations – local and international ones) and private sector firms, such as insurance companies. Business historians need to assess to what extent labour-intensive processes were co-ordinated by markets, networks and firms. The political-economy implications of labour-intensive industrialization also need to be examined.

Ideally, historians will be able to write up case studies of particular firms: to explore how in the 1950s small workshops used tools and machinery, and how they recruited, trained and retained labour; and to assess whether they continued to use labour-intensive techniques into the 1960s (during the epoch of industrialization) and from the 1970s (during an epoch characterized by de-industrialization). On uncovering new micro-level sources, historians may find that the theory used in this article needs to be rewritten, and its applications re-thought. Business historians should try and answer certain questions in particular. Were workshops in the 1950s already using portable battery-powered machinery? Had they installed small petrol driven generators? Were they using energy sources efficiently? Theorists should also assess whether labour-intensive industrialization could provide solutions to the two central issues of twenty-first century political economy: how to reduce global poverty; and how to manage climate change.

## Conclusions

Quantitative and qualitative sources on industrialization in Hong Kong are scarce. New empirical evidence described here confirms that most units of production in 1950s Hong Kong were small, and that organizational dualism was a defining characteristic of industrialization: there were larger factories using power-driven machinery, and numerous smaller workshops using more traditional, labour-intensive techniques. As the latter were not counted by the Labour Department, and as bureaucratic procedures for the collection of raw data shifted over time, it is difficult to plot, time-series trends. However, cross-sectional analysis suggests that from the 1950s to the 1970s a quarter of industrial employees worked in enterprises employing less than twenty people. New quantitative and survey data (on the rattan ware furniture and basket ware; and umbrella making) confirm that organizational dualism was a defining feature of industrialization, and show that factories and workshops operated at different stages of production cycles. These findings, however, need to be verified by micro studies that show how exactly small scale enterprises used labour and machinery in the 1950s; and how, crucially, the use of modern and traditional technologies shifted over time. We need to know in particular how small workshops responded to rising wages in the 1960s and 1970s.

## Acknowledgements

This article derives from a project entitled 'Industry and institutions: Hong Kong', funded by the Leverhulme Trust (RF&G/3/RFG/2002/0276) and aided by archivists at the Public Record Office, Hong Kong; the National Archives, Kew, London; and the National Archives, Maryland, USA. It was informed by the work of K. Sugihara on 'labour-intensive' industrialization, and aided by comments from two anonymous referees.

### Notes

[1] UK, National Archives, CO859/1160, 'The Trade Union movement and the industrial situation in Hong Kong', P. C. M. Sedgewick, the Commissioner of Labour, 8 Jan. 1957; HK, PRO, HKRS41/1/1778, telegram from Governor of Hong Kong to Secretary of State for the Colonies, no. 433, 31 Dec. 1952.

[2] US, NA, RG89/846.G, Foreign Service Despatch, American Consulate General, Hong Kong, to the Department of State, Washington, no. 971, 20 Dec 1955: 'Hong Kong Rattan Furniture and Basketware Industry'; and HK, PRO, HKRS843/1/20: 'The Rattan Trade in Hong Kong', by David Lin, assistant labour officer, 3 May 1958.

[3] HK, PRO, HKRS843/1/20, 'The Umbrella Industry and Trade in Hong Kong', by Sylvia Wong Mei-yee, Assistant labour officer, 23 May 1962; HKRS163/1/2749/16/70, 'The umbrella and umbrella parts industry', 21 May 1970.

[4] HKRS1017/2/1, Memorandum from E. C. Brown, Labour Officer, to the Commissioner of Labour, 28 Nov. 1958.

[5] US, NA, RG59 (Economic 1960–63) 846G, John Lacey, Consul Hong Kong, to the Department of State, no. 474, March 2 1960.

# References

Benham, F. C. (1956) The growth of manufacturing in Hong Kong, *International Affairs*, pp. 456–463.

Braga, J. M. (Ed.) (1957) *Hong Kong Business Symposium* (Hong Kong: South China Morning Post).

Brown, R. A. (Ed.) (1996) *Chinese Business Enterprise* (London: Routledge).

Chandler, A. D. (1990) *Scale and Scope: The Dynamics of Industrial.* Capitalism (Boston: Belknap Press of Harward University Press).

Chen, E. K. Y. & Li, K-w. (1988) Industry, in: H. C. Y. Ho & L. C. Chau (Eds) *The Economic System of Hong Kong*, pp. 113–139 (Hong Kong: Centre for Asian Studies).

Cheng, L. & Hsiung, P-c. (1998) Engendering the 'Economic Miracle': the Labour Market in the Asia-Pacific, in: G. Thompson (Ed.) *Economic Dynamism in the Asia Pacific: the Growth of Integration and Competitiveness*, pp. 112–137 (London and New York: Routledge).

Choi, C-c. (1998) Kinship and business: paternal and materal kin in Chaozhou Chinese family firms, *Business History*, 40(1), pp. 26–49.

Chow, S. C-m. (1977) Economic growth and income distribution in Hong Kong, Unpublished Ph.D. thesis: Boston University.

Clayton, D. (1997) *Imperialism Revisited: Political and Economic Relations Between Britain and China, 1950–54* (London: Macmillan).

Clayton, D. (2000i) A Hong Kong knitting factory in 1933: its reconstruction from bankruptcy court records, *Journal of Industrial History*, 3(2), pp. 51–70.

Clayton, D. W. (2000ii) Industrialization and institutional change in Hong Kong, 1842–1960, in: A. J. H. Latham & H. Kawakatsu (Eds) *Asia Pacific Dynamism 1550–2000*, pp. 149–169 (London: Routledge).

Clayton, D. (2004) The consumption of radio broadcast technologies in Hong Kong, c.1930–1960, *Economic History Review*, LVII(4), pp. 691–726.

Clayton, D. W. (forthcoming) From 'free trade' to 'fair trade': the transfer of employment law to colonial Hong Kong, 1958–62, *Journal of Imperial and Commonwealth History*.

Economist Intelligence Unit Limited (1962) Industry in Hong Kong. Hong Kong: report for the Federation of Hong Kong Industries.

England, J. & Rear, R. (1975) *Chinese Labour under British Rule, A Critical Study of Labour Relations and Law in Hong Kong*, pp. 53–59 (Hong Kong: Oxford University Press).

Epsy, J. L. (1974) The strategy of Chinese industrial enterprise in Hong Kong. Unpublished DBA dissertation (Boston: Harvard University).

Francks, P. (1999) *Japanese Economic Development: theory and practice* (London and New York: Routledge).

Hamilton, G. (Ed.) (1996) *Asian Business Networks and Economic Development in East and Southeast Asia* (Hong Kong: Centre of Asian Studies, University of Hong Kong).

Lee, K-M. (1999) Flexible manufacturing in a colonial economy, in: T-w. Ngo (Ed.) *Hong Kong's History: State and society under colonial rule*, pp. 162–180 (London: Routledge).

Leeming, F. (1975) The early industrialization of Hong Kong, *Modern Asian Studies*, 9(3), pp. 337–342.

Meyer, D. R. (2000) *Hong Kong as a Global Metropolis* (Cambridge: Cambridge University Press).

Ngo, T-W. (1999) Industrial history and the artifice of *Laissez-faire* colonialism, in: Ngo (Ed.) *Hong Kong's History: State and Society under Colonial Rule*, pp. 119–141 (London: Routledge).

Nthenda, L. (1979) Recent trends in government and industry relationship in Hong Kong, in: T-B. Lin, R. P. L. Lee & U-d. Simonis (Eds) *Hong Kong Economic, Social and Political Studies in Development*, pp. 167–183 (New York: Sharpe).

Podmore, D. (1971) The population of Hong Kong, in: K. Hopkins (Ed.) *Hong Kong: the Industrial Colony*, pp. 21–55 (Hong Kong: Oxford University Press).

Redding, S. G. (1990) *The Spirit of Chinese Capitalism* (Berlin: Walter de Gryuter).

Riedel, J. (1974) *The Industrialization of Hong Kong* (Tübingen: J.C. Mohr (Paul Siebeck)).

Roy, T. (1993) *Artisans and Industrialization. Indian Weaving in the Twentieth century* (Delhi: Oxford University Press).

Sabel, C. F. & Zeitlin, J. (Eds) (1997) *World of Possibilities: flexible and mass production in Western Industrialisation* (Cambridge: Cambridge University Press).

Sit, V. F-s. (1979) *Small Scale Industry in a Laissez-Faire Economy: A Hong Kong Case Study: a Comparative Project on Small Manufacturing Enterprise Organisation by the Association of Development Research and Training Institute of Asia and the Pacific* (Hong Kong: Centre of Asian Studies, University of Hong Kong).

de Soto, H. (2000) *The Mystery of Capital: Why Capitalism Triumphs in the West and Fails Everywhere Else* (New York: Basic Books).

Sugihara, K. (2003) The East Asian path of economic development: a long term perspective, in: A. Arrighi, T. Hamashita & M. Selden (Eds) *The Resurgence of East Asia: 500, 150 and 50 Year Perspectives* (London: Routledge).

Sugihara, K. (2004) The State and the Industrious Revolution in Tokugawa Japan (London: London School of Economic and Political Science Working Paper No. 02/04).

Szcepanik, E. (1958) *The Economic Growth of Hong Kong* (London: Oxford University Press).

Thirlwall, A. P. (1994) *Growth and Development* (London: Macmillan).

Wong, S-l. (1988) *Emigrant Entrepreneurs: Shanghai Industrialists in Hong Kong* (Hong Kong: Oxford University Press).

Young, A. (1989) Hong Kong and the Art of Landing of One's Feet: a Case Study of a Structurally Flexible Economy, Tuffs University, Fletcher School of Law and Diplomacy, Ph.D.

Yu, T. F-u. (1997) *Entrepreneurship and Economic Development in Hong Kong* (London: Routledge).

# What can we Conclude About Changing Trade, Capital and Management Across Asia?

CHRIS ROWLEY

The chapters in this volume concentrated on the importance of, and changes in, trade, capital markets, foreign direct investment (FDI), industry, types/forms/size of organisation and business such as multinational companies (MNCs), management and economic development across varied Asian economies. The countries covered included those in South East and North East Asia, such as Thailand, Malaysia, Indonesia, the Philippines Japan, Korea and China (and Hong Kong), These were analysed in a variety of ways and in a usefully comparative and historically grounded fashion.

What can we conclude? What did each of the chapter's conclude? The first chapter, by Edsel L. Beja, Jr., 'Was Capital Fleeing Southeast Asia? Estimates from Indonesia, Malaysia, The Philippines, and Thailand', was concerned with capital fleeing South East Asia. It concluded that Indonesia, Malaysia, the Philippines and Thailand experienced substantial capital flight between 1970 and 2002. As expected, capital flight was high during periods of crises, but it found also that there were cases when flight was high during periods of economic growth and increased in periods of deregulation and financial liberalization. The significant amounts of lost resources therein could have been used in the domestic economy to actually generate more output and additional jobs, thus producing better quality economic growth and ultimately social welfare improvement. To address this capital flight issue the chapter argued that some policies needed to be in situ. First, governments could pursue policies that strengthened macroeconomic performance and macro-organisational fundamentals. Second, governments needed to be embedded in their societies and promoting domestic responsibility in setting economic targets and articulating a vision of economic development taking into account domestic characteristics and contexts. Third, governments could institute capital management techniques to retain capital in domestic economies and direct resources into productive uses. Fourth, there was a need for better management of external debts by debtors and creditors alike.

With a general perception of China 'threatening' industry, globally, the second chapter, by Yushi Yoshida and Hiro Ito's 'How do the Asian Economies Compete with Japan in the US Market? Is China Exceptional? A Triangular Trade Approach', argued that while US current account deficits had grown recently, China had expanded its current account surpluses against the US. Many claimed that China manipulated its currency values to keep it at an unfairly low level against the US dollar. This chapter shed light on the trade disputes from a different angle and presented results with important political ramifications. Thus, a surge in Chinese exports to the US involved a large volume of products manufactured by Japanese affiliates in China, therefore, reflecting Japanese MNC global production strategies, not so much the 'threat' of Chinese industrialization. Thus, even if China changed exchange rate policy and re-valued its currency or let it completely float, foreign MNCs could continue exporting their products from China. Thus, it seems to be that only some weakening of MNC incentives to produce in China may mitigate trade imbalances. Also, any decline in Chinese exports to the US was likely to be matched by increased exports from other parts of the world. Again, it seemed to be MNCs that really matter in this.

The third chapter, Paul Lejot, Douglas Arner and Liu Qiao 'Missing Links: Regional Reforms for Asia's Bond Markets', noted that Asia's debt capital markets were of limited use to many potential participants as they failed to induce issuance of sufficient depth and risk quality to satisfy investors and provided little guard against financial shocks. In particular, the chapter argued that Asia's 1997 Financial Crisis suggested that the region may become less prone to financial contagion by reducing reliance on its banking sectors for credit and intermediation, and improving efficiency in deploying savings. Asia was generally free from non-cyclical aggregate shortages of capital but its capability to apportion financial resources was suspect. Liquid debt securities markets existed comprehensively only in Japan, even though notes or bonds were issued in most countries and Asian international borrowers were well regarded, though not prolific. This chapter argued that active debt markets would improve national and regional resource allocation by providing an unbiased, visible price mechanism, widen the choice available to investors and diminish the contagion effects of market instability. However, such results required collaborative actions that represented unprecedented economic cooperation and tests of regional and bilateral institutions. The chapter described Asia's bond markets, their roots in funding patterns and the concerns of policymakers examining their future. It traced the origins of advanced markets, their legacy for developing economies, and suggested prescriptive lessons using research into the interplay between legal systems and financial institutions. The chapter concluded with proposals amenable to national interests and the nascent objectives of regional financial policy. It argued that the chapter's suggested proposals were not mutually exclusive. The simplest means to remove obstacles to development (Proposal 1) was to permit a collaborative offshore market for which from inception no impediment could exist (2), as seen elsewhere. Second, permitting an offshore market would facilitate the speedy introduction of more complex mechanisms to allow securitization on the broadest scale (3), even without legal changes. Active markets would exist only with governmental commitment to reform, providing all commitments were market orientated. These proposals favoured open price mechanisms in an institutional sense and should not be taken as suggesting that bank-centred or market-centred systems were intrinsically superior, nor that the means by which financial sector reform was introduced could be universal.

In the fourth chapter, Andrew Atherton and Alaric Fairbanks 'Stimulating Private Sector Development in China: The Emergence of Enterprise Development Centres in Liaoning and Sichuan Provinces', argued that enterprise development centres were examples of an emergent form of institution in China that reflected the changing nature of the economy and its organisation, particularly in terms of the role that government played in economic development. With the withdrawal of state management of enterprises via the transfers of ownership of township and village enterprises and smaller state-owned enterprises, the Chinese economy had become increasingly dominated by the private sector. The shift in focus by government towards developing a small number of 'national champions' owned by the state indicated that the rest of the economy would become more removed from public ownership, and hence from direct government control. This trend suggested a very different relationship between state and markets than existed before 1978 when almost all businesses were publicly-owned and national economic activity was essentially part of the state. Within such a scenario the prospects and paths of development and growth of the private sector had become more important as it accounted for an increased share of national output. At the same time the government's relationship with businesses and the ways in which it encouraged and supported their development were liable to change. In mixed economies where the private sector accounted for most economic activity and output, governments tended to establish and support 'intermediary' institutions that could work with, and enable the development and growth of the private sector. Business development and support institutions were seen, as a result, as integral to economic development. Thus, the Chinese centres were models of, and experiments in, establishing intermediary institutions whose remit was to support and stimulate the development of the private sector in a country where rapid and sustained economic growth had historically suppressed the need for such institutions. The establishment of these new institutions occurred as the private sector had grown and government had started to withdraw from direct ownership and management of most enterprises. This thesis suggested that the enterprise development centres would become a conduit for the allocation and provision of government, and perhaps social, resources to stimulate economic development through private sector growth and expansion. The chapter also pointed to the possibility that these institutions would become increasingly important to the future economic development of China should overall rates of growth slow and government began seeking out strategies for stimulating new forms of economic expansion – a characteristic of industrial policy in mature economies.

Chapter 5, by Christopher Wright and Seung-Ho Kwon 'Business Crisis and Management Fashion: Korean Companies, Restructuring and Consulting Advice', demonstrated that the concept of management fashion, while a useful construct in analysing management knowledge diffusion, needed to take greater account of the role of varying institutional, cultural and organisational contexts. Far from there being a one-way flow from fashion setter to fashion consumer, this chapter demonstrated how varying contexts could at different times both impede and assist management knowledge diffusion. Fashion setters, such as consultants, were not free agents and were themselves dependent on the reactions of their consumer market. Thus, managers and employees as consumers of management fashions may well reject the attempts of foreign fashion setters to sell innovations that fail to fit with their business environment or adopt such innovations in a pragmatic and creative manner. By contrast, in circumstances where local practice was seen as problematic such alien innovations may be increasingly attractive simply because of their foreign nature. Teasing out these shifting dynamics and the circumstances under which the diffusion process was affected required further research in divergent social and economic settings it was argued. The recent expansion of management consulting in other Asian economies, such as China and India, offered further potential arenas in which to study the role of consultancies in diffusing management ideas and practices. There was also a need for more company-level case studies of how management knowledge was created and packaged by global consultancies for new and developing markets, and correspondingly how such fashions were received, interpreted and adapted by individual businesses within these markets the authors assert.

Finally, in Chapter 6, David Clayton 'Labour–Intensive Industrialization in Hong Kong, 1950–70: A Note on Sources and Methods', argued that quantitative and qualitative sources concerning industrialization in Hong Kong were scarce. New empirical evidence described in this chapter confirmed that most units of production in 1950s Hong Kong were small and that organisational dualism was a defining characteristic of industrialisation: there were larger factories using power-driven machinery but also numerous smaller workshops using more traditional, labour intensive techniques. However, as the latter were not counted (by the Labour Department) and as bureaucratic procedures for the collection of raw data shifted over time, it was difficult to plot time-series trends. Nevertheless, cross-sectional analysis suggested that the 1950s–70s saw 23 per cent of industrial employees in enterprises employing less than 20 people. New quantitative and survey data (on the rattan ware furniture and basket ware; and umbrella making used here) confirmed that such organizational dualism was a feature of Hong Kong industrialisation, and showed that factories and workshops operated at different stages of production cycles. These findings, however, needed to be verified by micro studies that showed how exactly small scale enterprises used labour and machinery in the 1950s; and how, crucially, the use of modern and traditional technologies shifted over time the author argued. We need to know in particular how small workshops responded to rising wages in the 1960s and 1970s the chapter concluded.

Reading these chapters shows that a strong institutional establishment and legal framework are pre-requisites for management, success in trade and industrial development. Also, this collection shows the importance of disaggregated and detailed research and data to get below the surface and veneer of some debates. For example, the common assertion that it is China that is somehow decimating the economies of the West and the global economy, whereas it may well be foreign MNCs based in China. Similarly, we can question the constraints and bounded nature of the presumptive omnipotence of managerial fashions and consultants. As such, the changing patterns of trade, capital, organisation and management should not been seen in a conceptual, spatial or historical vacuum, but rather within the rich grounded cultural, institutional and organizational context.

# INDEX